TECHNOLOGY IN ANCIENT CULTURES

ANCIENT

COMMUNICATION

TECHNOLOGY

FROM HIEROGLYPHICS TO SCROLLS

Michael Woods and
Mary B. Woods

Twenty-First Century Books · Minneapolis

For Glenn Ruskin and Nancy Blount,
great modern communicators

Twenty-First Century Books
A division of Lerner Publishing Group, Inc.
241 First Avenue North
Minneapolis, MN 55401 U.S.A.

Website address: www.lernerbooks.com

Library of Congress Cataloging-in-Publication Data

Woods, Michael, 1946–
        Ancient communication technology : from hieroglyphics to scrolls / by Michael Woods and Mary B. Woods.
            p.   cm. — (Technology in ancient cultures)
        Includes bibliographical references and index.
        ISBN 978-0-7613-6529-7 (lib. bdg. : alk. paper)
            1. Nonverbal communication—History—To 1500—Juvenile literature. 2. Signals and signaling—History—to 1500—
    Juvenile literature. I. Woods, Mary B. (Mary Boyle), 1946– II. Title.
        P99.5.W665 2011
        302.2'2209—dc22   2010025487

Manufactured in the United States of America
1 – PC – 12/31/10

TABLE OF CONTENTS

4   INTRODUCTION

8   CHAPTER ONE
COMMUNICATION BASICS

18 CHAPTER TWO
THE ANCIENT MIDDLE EAST

26 CHAPTER THREE
ANCIENT EGYPT

34 CHAPTER FOUR
ANCIENT INDIA

40 CHAPTER FIVE
ANCIENT CHINA

48 CHAPTER SIX
THE ANCIENT AMERICAS

58 CHAPTER SEVEN
ANCIENT GREECE

68 CHAPTER EIGHT
ANCIENT ROME

76 EPILOGUE
AFTER THE ANCIENTS

84   Timeline   91   Further Reading
86   Glossary   93   Websites
88   Source Notes   94   Index
90   Selected Bibliography

THE ANCIENT WORLDS OF COMMUNICATION

EUROPE

ASIA

GERMANY

Vallon-
Pont-d'Arc
Altamira

FRANCE

Rome

SPAIN

ANCIENT
GREECE

Pergamum
Athens

TURKEY

LEBANON

SYRIA

Euphrates
R.

ANCIENT
MIDDLE
EAST

Samarkand

Tigris R.

Indus
R.

ANCIENT
CHINA

NORTH
KOREA

SOUTH
KOREA

JAPAN

ANCIENT
INDIA

QIN
DYNASTY

Sparta
Mediterranean Sea

IRAQ

Susa

Alexandria

ISRAEL

Uruk

ROMAN
EMPIRE

Deir el-Medina

ANCIENT
EGYPT

Nile
R.

AFRICA

INDIAN OCEAN

ATLANTIC
OCEAN

AUSTRALIA

INTRODUCTION

What do you think of when you hear the word *technology*? You probably think of something totally new. You might think of research laboratories filled with computers, powerful microscopes, and other scientific tools. But *technology* doesn't refer only to brand-new machines and discoveries. Technology is as old as human society.

Technology is the use of knowledge, inventions, and discoveries to make life better. The word *technology* comes from two Greek words. One, *techne*, means "art" or "craft." The other, *logos*, means "logic" or "reason." Ancient Greeks originally used the word *technology* to mean a discussion of arts and crafts. In modern times, the word usually refers to an art or craft itself.

▲ Modern technology, such as this sleek digital tablet, allows people to create, access, and share information instantaneously and globally.

There are many forms of technology. Medicine is one form. Agriculture and machinery are others. This book looks at a form of technology that helps make all other kinds of technology possible: communication.

To communicate is to share news, ideas, feelings, and images with other people. Communication involves more than just speaking, writing, and reading. It includes art, music, and other nonverbal forms of sharing information. It also includes the equipment people use to share information. Paper, pens, ink, paintbrushes, and books are all forms of communication technology.

WORD TRAVELS

The story of communication is the story of human society. The first humans on Earth moved from place to place, looking for fresh sources of food. Once the earliest humans started communicating, they were able to settle disputes, cooperate with each other, and plan ahead. Around 10,000 B.C., humans began to settle into permanent villages. As villages grew into cities, life became more complicated. People needed reliable ways of keeping records. They developed writing systems.

Ancient peoples developed new communication technology by trial and error. Sometimes they copied communication technology invented in other countries and added their own new touches. The ancient Phoenicians lived in modern-day Syria and Lebanon. They borrowed an early written alphabet from other Middle Eastern peoples. Later groups such as the Greeks, the Etruscans, and the Romans borrowed from the Phoenicians. They all added their own changes and improvements to the alphabet.

People who lived thousands of years ago developed our most basic communication tools. The ancient Chinese made paper from wood pulp more than 1,900 years ago. The ancient Greeks and Romans wrote stories, poems, and plays that modern people still study. Some ancient civilizations even developed postal systems. Archaeologists, scientists who study the remains of past cultures, continue to make new discoveries about the history of human communication.

This book reveals how advances in communication improved ancient life. Read on and discover the communication technology that helped move the world forward.

CHAPTER ONE

COMMUNICATION BASICS

The first humans on Earth lived about 2.5 million years ago. They were hunters and gatherers. They lived in small groups and got their food by hunting game, fishing, and gathering wild plants. When the food in one area was all used up, the group moved to a new place. Hunter-gatherers made tools from stone, wood, animal bones, plant fibers, and clay. In some places on Earth, the hunter-gatherer lifestyle remained unchanged until only a few centuries ago.

▼ Some early peoples depicted human–animal interactions on the walls of caves. This seventeen-thousand-year-old cave art from Lascaux, France, shows a person, perhaps a hunter *(left)*, and a bison.

The earliest humans communicated with grunts, growls, and physical gestures long before they made words—specific sounds to stand for specific objects or ideas. They may have tried to imitate sounds they heard in nature, such as animal calls or the boom of thunder. Simple noises and movements were most likely quite effective ways to share information. Early humans lived in small groups. People all knew each other very well. In many areas, contact with strangers was rare. In such tight-knit units it would have been easy to guess what another person meant by a grunt or wave of the hand.

HOW SPEECH STARTED

Human speech developed slowly. Our prehuman ancestors had mouths and throats suited mainly for chewing, swallowing, and breathing. Their larynxes (the voice boxes that contain vocal cords) were too high in their throats to make a wide range of noises. Over thousands of years, human brains grew larger. The human skull changed shape. People gained the ability to produce the sounds that made up ancient languages.

Researchers who study the growth of speech face many challenges. The earliest humans did not have writing systems. We do not know how their languages were structured or what words they used. Researchers also cannot study the speech organs of ancient peoples, such as the tongue or the larynx. These organs usually decay quickly after people die.

◀ Humans developed the ability to speak over a long period of time. Their brains grew larger and their skulls changed shape in ways that allowed for speech.

THE TALKING ANIMAL

Animals communicate with barks, squawks, hisses, and other utterances. These sounds can serve as mating calls, requests for food, or even warnings. For instance, a songbird's cry in spring may mean, "Stay out of my territory!"

Although some animal sounds carry meaning, humans are the only animals who carry on conversations. Through spoken language, early peoples passed on information, shared ideas, organized activities, and cooperated with others on projects that could not be done by one person alone. They discussed the past and planned for the future.

In 2007 scientists discovered the remains of a prehuman hyoid bone (jawbone) dating from about three hundred thousand years ago. The bone is similar to those of modern humans. Discoveries such as this one have led some scholars to wonder if our prehuman ancestors communicated through an early form of speech. But other scholars have noted that the brains of these early humans may not have been advanced enough for them to make full use of speech organs. Some scientists think that speech developed only about fifty thousand years ago, when people began living in groups.

CAVE PAINTINGS

The earliest humans probably screamed, smiled, cried, and shoved to get their messages across. This kind of communication lasted only a moment, then disappeared. Symbols made communication more permanent. With a painting or drawing, people could relay the same message time and again. Symbols encouraged people to remember experiences and record them for others to understand. Cave paintings mark a time when early peoples started to communicate with more than just sounds and actions.

One morning in 1879, Marcelino Sanz de Sautuola took his young daughter, Maria, to explore a cave near their home in Altamira in northern Spain. Sanz de Sautuola was a lawyer by trade but had a strong interest in history and geology. He had visited the cave before to study animal bones and stone tools he'd found on the cave floor. While Sanz de Sautuola worked, Maria wandered farther into the cave. She found a stretch of cave wall covered with colored drawings of bison, horses, and other animals that had not lived in Spain for thousands of years.

Sanz de Sautuola rightly guessed that the cave paintings were from the Paleolithic era, which began 2.5 million years ago and ended more than ten thousand years ago. Experts believe the paintings are about fourteen thousand years old. The Sanz de Sautuolas' discovery was the first of many.

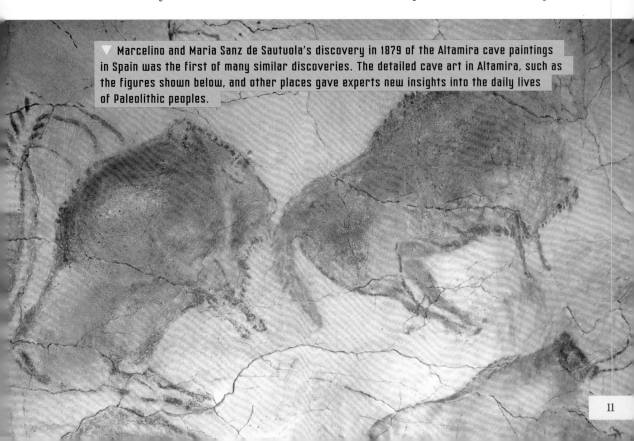

▼ Marcelino and Maria Sanz de Sautuola's discovery in 1879 of the Altamira cave paintings in Spain was the first of many similar discoveries. The detailed cave art in Altamira, such as the figures shown below, and other places gave experts new insights into the daily lives of Paleolithic peoples.

"Mira, Papa, bueyes [Look, Papa, oxen]!"

—Maria Sanz de Sautuola, daughter of Marcelino Sanz de Sautuola, upon seeing the Altamira cave paintings, 1879

In the following decades, other explorers discovered cave art in different parts of the world. The Altamira caves became world-famous.

Some of the oldest known cave paintings come from the wall of a cave in southern France. The cave, which is called the Chauvet Cave, is near the French town of Vallon-Pont-d'Arc. It contains more than three hundred paintings, all created between thirty-two thousand and thirty thousand years ago. Many of the paintings include beautiful images of bears, lions, horses, and wild cats. Some painters used natural bumps and grooves on cave walls to represent parts of animals' bodies.

One striking image from the Chauvet Cave shows a creature that is part animal, part human. The creature stands upright like a human but has the head, horns, and arched back of a bison. Archaeologists have taken to calling this creature the Sorcerer. But they aren't sure what it represented to the cave's ancient painters.

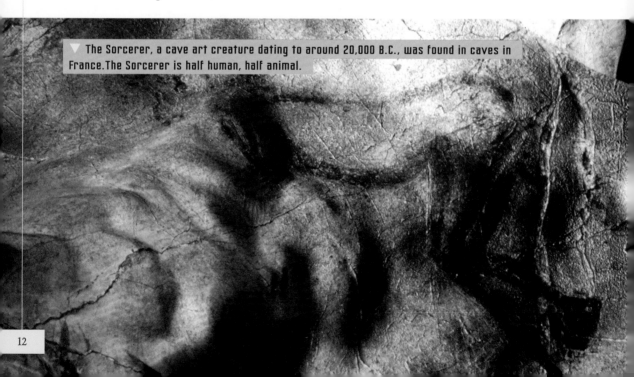

▼ The Sorcerer, a cave art creature dating to around 20,000 B.C., was found in caves in France. The Sorcerer is half human, half animal.

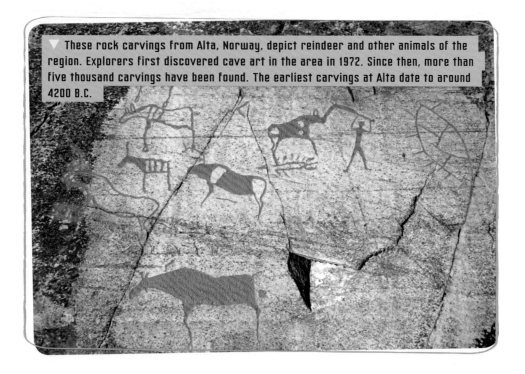

These rock carvings from Alta, Norway, depict reindeer and other animals of the region. Explorers first discovered cave art in the area in 1972. Since then, more than five thousand carvings have been found. The earliest carvings at Alta date to around 4200 B.C.

HOW DO WE KNOW?

Archaeologists have several ways of finding out the ages of cave paintings. In some cases, paintings show animals that are extinct (no longer living), such as woolly rhinoceroses. From studying fossils (the preserved remains of ancient animals) and other evidence, scientists know when woolly rhinoceroses died out. So they also know that an illustration of a woolly rhinoceros must have been made before that time.

Other paintings show animals that no longer live in an area. For instance, reindeer used to live in regions of Europe and Asia that eventually became too warm for the animals. The change in climate caused the reindeer to move further north. When scientists find a painting of a reindeer in a place where reindeer no longer live, they know that the painting was made before the climate changed.

Scientists also date paintings by testing charcoal, bones, and other materials that artists left inside caves. Analyzing these materials is often the best way to find a specific date rather than a close estimate.

MAGICAL PAINTINGS

Early peoples faced real danger to enter and paint inside caves. Many cave entrances are small and hard to find. Painters probably had to crawl great distances to reach some cave chambers. They likely walked through dark passages, guided only by stone lamps filled with burning animal fat. Caves were often home to dangerous bears, lions, bats, snakes, and bloodsucking insects. Cave painting must have been very important to ancient humans for so many people to take such risks.

Some scholars think that ancient cave painters were attempting to practice magic. Perhaps they painted scenes of hunters killing mastodons as a way to ask gods or spirits for a successful hunt. Or perhaps they believed that by painting the animals they were gaining a form of control over them. Some scholars have even suggested that the paintings were a way of praying for the survival of a species that hunters relied on for food.

Archaeologists have found hollow animal bones that were used to hold paint. People may have thought that paint stored in a mastodon bone contained the animal's spirit—and that it could bring luck to the hunters.

EARLY PAINTING TECHNIQUES

A person's finger most likely served as the first paintbrush. The earliest cave paintings show thick lines of paint. Ancient painters probably dipped their fingers into paint and then rubbed them on cave walls. But some lines in cave paintings are too thin to have been made with a finger. Archaeologists think that ancient painters made these marks with sharpened sticks or bird feathers. The painters used the sticks and feathers like quill pens.

People in ancient Argentina left these painted hands on cave walls more than 9,000 years ago. In modern times, we know the site of the paintings as the Cueva de las Manos (Cave of the Hands).

The first paintbrush might have been a twig. An artist probably chewed the end of the twig to separate its fibers. Once dry, the fibers worked like bristles to spread paint along cave walls. Painters also used brushes made from animal hair. They also dipped wads of fur or moss in paint and pressed the wads against cave walls.

In some caves, archaeologists have found outlines of human hands surrounded by sprayed paint. Ancient painters had more than one way to create a spray painting. Sometimes an artist placed a hand on a rock surface, took a mouthful of paint, and sprayed it out between the lips. Other times, painters used hollow reeds or bone pipes to blow paint against a wall.

Ancient cave painters used many of the same techniques for more than twenty thousand years. Because of the similarities between paintings across time, archaeologists believe that families and other small groups passed painting techniques down through generations.

ANCIENT PAINT

To make paint, early peoples used minerals and other natural substances. A rock made of iron oxide left a red mark when scratched on a cave wall. A rock made of manganese oxide left a black mark. Other rocks left blue-black, dark brown, or white marks. By grinding minerals into powder and mixing them with water, early peoples made liquid paints.

Soot from fires made a deep black paint when mixed with water. Berries and other plant parts provided more colors. Some ancient paints were very durable. We can still see the remains of cave paintings done more than thirty thousand years ago.

Cave artists made images with other dry materials such as charcoal, which comes from burned wood. Some ancient artists drew with calcium carbonate, a form of limestone also known as chalk. Chunks of chalk, scraped against a stone surface, left grayish-white marks, much like the chalk used on school blackboards.

ENGRAVINGS

Many ancient drawings were made by engraving. This technique involves cutting lines into a surface such as a cave wall or a piece of stone, bone, or antler. One

▲ Archaeologists found the Ishango bone in 1960 in central Africa. The bone *(front and back shown)* from a baboon's upper thigh was carved with notches. Many scientists think the bone, which dates to around 20,000 B.C., is probably a tally stick, although it's not clear what the notches were supposed to track. Some believe its grouped notches stand for a pattern of some sort—possibly a calendar of the moon's phases.

thirty-thousand-year-old bone features carvings that seem to record the phases of the moon—the changing appearance of the moon in the sky each night.

To make the lines, early peoples used a tool called a burin. The burin was a piece of very hard rock, such as flint, with a sharp tip. Archaeologists have found worn and broken flint burins on the ground right below ancient engravings.

Early artists also created images by pecking or chipping away bits of rock to form outlines. They probably pressed pointed stones to walls, bones, or other surfaces and tapped them carefully with stone hammers. Artists may have drawn outlines first with chalk and then chipped away bits of rock along the patterns. These engravings took a long time to make. Most have been found on flat, horizontal surfaces, where an artist could sit comfortably while working.

Some ancient artists combined painting and engraving to create a beautiful new form of communication. The artists began by engraving an outline or image on a rock surface. Then they applied a thin coat of paint that made the engraved lines more visible. The Sorcerer of Chauvet Cave is one example of a colored engraving.

▶ A detail of a colored stone engraving from Scandinavia shows human figures rowing ships. This rock engraving from around 1500 B.C. is at the Viking Ship Museum in Oslo, Norway.

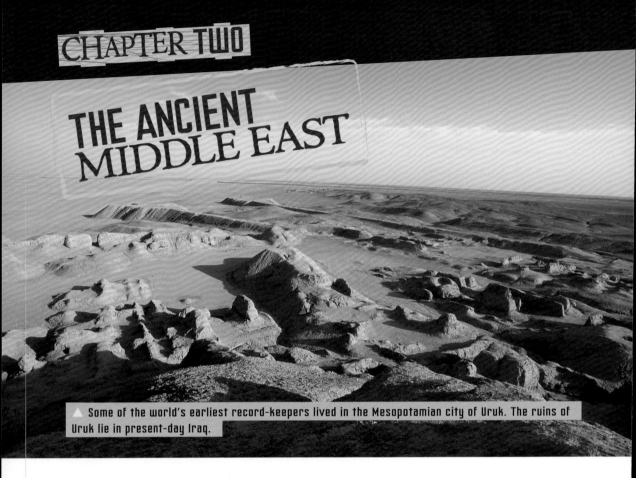

CHAPTER TWO

THE ANCIENT MIDDLE EAST

▲ Some of the world's earliest record-keepers lived in the Mesopotamian city of Uruk. The ruins of Uruk lie in present-day Iraq.

Between 10,000 and 3500 B.C., some ancient peoples abandoned the hunter-gatherer lifestyle. They began to farm and build permanent villages. Several distinct cultures developed in the ancient Middle East—the region where Asia, Africa, and Europe meet. Sumer is the earliest known civilization in the ancient Middle East or elsewhere. The Sumerians lived between the Tigris and Euphrates rivers in a region later named Mesopotamia (which means "between rivers" in Greek).

Mesopotamia included most of modern Iraq and parts of modern Syria and Turkey. The area was home to a series of civilizations, including the Babylonians, Hittites, and Assyrians. These groups were very successful at growing food. For the first time in history, humans had extra food—a surplus—that they could sell to others.

ONE TECHNOLOGY LEADS TO ANOTHER

As Middle Eastern peoples produced food and goods in greater amounts, they could no longer rely on brainpower alone to remember things. Government officials had to keep track of laws and who had paid taxes. Farmers needed records of how much land they owned and how much food they had produced. Merchants needed records of the goods they sold and debts owed to them. The need to keep records led to a new kind of communication technology—writing.

The first kind of writing was picture-writing. Pictures used for writing are called *pictographs*. Mesopotamian pictographs showed images from everyday life: grain, tools, fish, birds, and other animals and objects. Pictographs also expressed action, like the verbs in modern writing. For instance, a picture of a person's mouth combined with a picture of food meant "eat." A picture of an eye accompanied by lines or dots stood for crying. A picture of a foot next to a picture of mountains stood for traveling to the mountains.

WRITING ON TABLETS

Mesopotamia had lots of high-quality clay. People used the clay to make building materials such as bricks. By the fourth millennium B.C. they were also using it to store information. Mesopotamians made records on small, smooth pieces of clay called tablets. When a clay tablet was damp, a person could scratch pictures and letters into its surface using a sharpened reed. The writer let the clay dry and harden in the hot sun to preserve the writing. Archaeologists have found many tablets from ancient Mesopotamia that are still in very good condition.

Some of the earliest known written records come from the Mesopotamian city of Uruk in present-day Iraq. Archaeologists have found clay tablets in Uruk dating to between 3300 and 2900 B.C. Most tablets document the trading of food and livestock. Other tablets list the names of animals or important officials.

Until the mid-twentieth century, experts wondered if a single person from Uruk, or perhaps a group of merchants, invented writing. But archaeologists have discovered tablets with ancient forms of writing in other areas of the Middle East. These tablets also date to the late 3000s B.C.

▼ This Sumerian clay tablet dates to between 3100 and 2900 B.C. The tablet was most likely used by a government official to record the exchange of food and goods.

In 1984 archaeologists found clay tablets in present-day Syria that may be older than the tablets from Uruk. The tablets include images of a goat and a sheep with a number next to each animal. Because of these findings, most experts believe that many people invented writing over a long period of time. The ancient record-keepers from Uruk may have based their writing systems on earlier models that scientists haven't discovered.

CUNEIFORM

Writing on wet clay was messy and difficult. The sharpened tips of reeds created big grooves with raised edges on the wet clay. These edges smeared easily.

This process might have frustrated the first writers in ancient Mesopotamia. Eventually they found a better way of recording data on wet clay. Writers

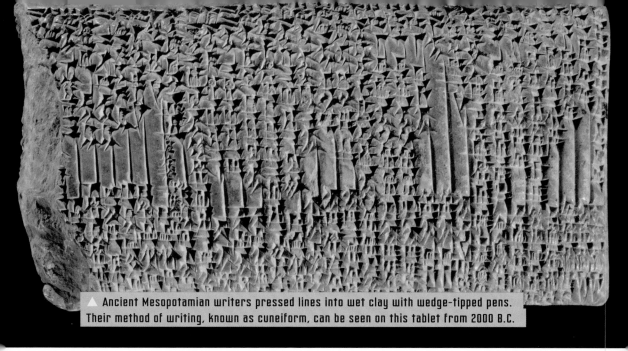

pressed lines straight down into clay with special wedge-tipped reed pens. The pens made indentations in the clay with no raised edges.

Later peoples named this manner of writing *cuneiform*, after the Latin term *cuneus*, which means "wedge." Middle Eastern peoples used cuneiform for at least fifteen different languages over more than three thousand years.

SO MANY SYMBOLS

Pictographs worked fairly well as symbols for familiar objects, but they weren't very good for describing new objects or complicated actions. Over time, pictographs slowly changed shape. They became abstract—meaning they no longer looked like the objects they represented. Instead, Middle Eastern writers had to memorize the meaning of each symbol—eventually more than two thousand in all.

Around 2800 B.C., people in the ancient Middle East began to use pictures to stand for sounds instead of for objects or ideas. They developed a syllabary—a set of written symbols that could be combined to form words. With a syllabary, people could write any word in a language. People could also invent new words to stand for new objects and ideas.

THE FIRST ALPHABET?

An alphabet is a set of letters used in writing a language. The symbols that make up an alphabet stand for more specific sounds than the symbols in a syllabary. Because we lack complete information about early writing systems, we don't know for sure what system contained the first alphabet.

Archaeologists have found inscriptions on bowls and other utensils in modern-day Palestine that date from between the sixteenth and thirteenth century B.C. The inscriptions belong to a writing system known as Proto-Canaanite, which is a precursor to various languages and writing systems such as Hebrew. Researchers have not fully decoded the Proto-Canaanite symbols, but some archaeologists believe that the Proto-Canaanite writing system led to the North Semitic alphabet.

The North Semitic alphabet is named after the Semites, people who once lived in modern-day Israel and Lebanon. Many of its letters are similar to Proto-Canaanite pictograms. But the North Semitic alphabet is closer in nature to modern alphabets than the earlier system. Peoples of the Middle East used this system in the eleventh century B.C. or earlier.

Near the start of the first millennium B.C., the Phoenicians adopted a form of the North Semitic alphabet. The Phoenicians developed a set of twenty-two letters that could be combined to express words. In time, other cultures borrowed from the Phoenician system as well.

THE EVOLUTION OF THE MODERN ALPHABET

Proto-Canaanite 16th–13th century B.C.	ⴷ	⊓	∟	⋈	Ψ	⌁	8
North Semitic 13th–11th century B.C.	ⱉ	⊼	⏋	◿	ⱻ	⌇	ⵁ
Phoenician 11th–9th century B.C.	Ɫ	⌐	∧	◁	⋑	ⱱ	ⵁ
Greek 9th century B.C.	A	B	Γ	Δ	E	M	ⵁ
Roman (modern) 7th century B.C.	A	B	C	D	E	M	Q

THE DEAD SEA SCROLLS

One day in 1947, a young shepherd was tending a flock of sheep in the rugged desert on the northwestern shore of the Dead Sea in modern-day Israel. The shepherd found the opening to a cave and began to explore the inside. He found ancient manuscripts that had been hidden away for almost two thousand years.

During the next twenty years, archaeologists found about nine hundred similar manuscripts in other caves nearby. Scholars named the manuscripts the Dead Sea Scrolls *(one of which is shown at right)*. The scrolls date to between 200 B.C. and A.D. 68. Many of the scrolls are copies of sections of the Hebrew Bible. Other scrolls reveal Jewish religious teachings that did not become part of the Bible. Still others describe the rules and beliefs of local Jewish communities from the ancient Middle East. The writers of the scrolls wrote in Hebrew, Aramaic, and Greek. They used several different materials for writing surfaces, such as on papyrus (a plant-based material similar to paper), animal hide, and sheets of copper.

The scrolls were one of the most important finds in modern archaeology. They gave scholars a wealth of new information about the origins of the Bible and life in the ancient Middle East. Many archaeologists believe that the Jews hid the scrolls in caves for safekeeping when the Roman army invaded the region between A.D. 66 and 73.

ANCIENT STORYTELLING

Ancient peoples used the new technology of writing not only for business and legal records, but also to entertain and to teach. One of the most famous ancient written works is the Hebrew Bible. The Hebrew Bible contains many teachings of the modern-day Jewish religion. It also serves as the Old Testament, the first part of the Christian Bible. The Hebrew Bible's first section, the book of Genesis, describes how the Hebrew god created the world.

Experts aren't sure how the Hebrew Bible developed or who wrote it. People in ancient Israel most likely shared the book's stories orally before anyone wrote the stories down. Most experts agree that multiple writers contributed to the Hebrew Bible over hundreds of years. The work contains information on the history and the people of Israel from the 1300s B.C. to the 100s B.C. Different sections of the Hebrew Bible feature different styles of writing.

Another written work, the *Epic of Gilgamesh,* was told throughout southern Mesopotamia as early as 2000 B.C. According to this story, Gilgamesh was a king from Sumer. He was a great warrior but a harsh ruler. The Mesopotamian god Anu sent a hero,

▲ Mesopotamian peoples began to put the *Epic of Gilgamesh* in writing by the seventeenth century B.C., the period to which this cuneiform tablet dates. Writing on the tablet describes the destructive flood at the tale's end.

> "Surpassing all kings, powerful and tall/
> beyond all others, violent, splendid,/
> a wild bull of a man, unvanquished leader,/
> hero in the front lines, beloved by his soldiers—/
> fortress they called him, *protector of the people,/
> raging flood that destroys all defenses.*"

— From the *Epic of Gilgamesh*, a Mesopotamian epic poem, ca. 2000 B.C.

Enkidu, to kill Gilgamesh. Instead, the two men became friends and shared many adventures. When Enkidu died, Gilgamesh became afraid of death. He searched for a way to live forever. In the end he failed, and a great flood destroyed everything in the world.

At first, Mesopotamian storytellers told the tale of Gilgamesh from memory. Later storytellers put the legend down on clay tablets. In 1853 a Turkish archaeologist discovered the most complete known written version at the ruins of an ancient palace in modern-day Iraq. He found a copy of the story, written in cuneiform on twelve tablets, in the palace library. The tablets date from the 600s B.C.

◄ An ancient relief carving from around 5000 B.C., found in modern-day Syria, shows a scene from the *Epic of Gilgamesh*. Gilgamesh himself is in the center, between two bull men.

CHAPTER THREE

ANCIENT EGYPT

▲ The yearly flooding of Egypt's Nile River made nearby soil suitable for growing grains, fruits, and papyrus plants. Papyrus was used in early papermaking.

Around 8000 B.C., northern Africa's wet climate became drier. Hunter-gatherers in the area began to move east, toward the Nile River in Egypt. The Nile flows for 4,145 miles (6,671 kilometers), making it the longest river in the world. By about 7000 B.C. people had built permanent settlements along the river. The Nile flooded its banks every July. The floodwater soaked the soil and deposited fertile, mudlike silt on the surrounding land.

Many plants grew along the shores of the Nile. Early Egyptian farmers raised wheat, barley, vegetables, and fruits. The papyrus plant also thrived in Egypt's fertile silt. With this plant, the ancient Egyptians changed the history of human communication.

PAPER FROM PAPYRUS

Papyrus grows in creeks and rivers. It sometimes grows as tall as 15 feet (4.6 m). The plant has a triangular stem that may be more than 2 inches (5 centimeters) wide. Ancient Egyptians turned these stems into an early form of paper.

Papermakers cut the stems into narrow strips and scraped away the inner layers of fiber. They placed several strips side by side, with the edges barely touching, to form a long, narrow rectangle. They spread shorter strips on top, at right angles to the strips beneath. Next, the papermakers wet the strips with water, beat them with hammers, and pressed them under heavy weights. The pressure sealed the two layers together. Papermakers left the sheets to dry and then polished them. The resulting pieces of papyrus were bright white and smooth.

Papermakers often glued together as many as twenty sheets to create rolls more than 30 feet (9 m) in length. When the rolls were made correctly, the seams between the pages were almost invisible.

▼ This papyrus illustration depicts figures from Egyptian mythology.

> ## "The nature of papyrus too is to be recounted [told], for on its use as rolls human civilization depends, at the most for its life, and certainly for its memory."

—Pliny the Elder, Roman philosopher and politician, *Naturalis Historia*, A.D. 706

The earliest known example of paper made from papyrus dates to around 3100 B.C. Archaeologists discovered this papyrus in an ancient Egyptian tomb. From Egypt, papyrus spread to other ancient countries. It had reached Greece by the sixth or seventh century B.C. and Rome after that. But the material was expensive and precious. Egyptian rulers tightly controlled the trading of papyrus paper. The English word *papyrus* may originate with the Egyptian word *pa-en-per-aa*—"the material of Pharoah (king)."[3]

SACRED CARVINGS

The Egyptian system of picture writing, hieroglyphics, is one of the most recognizable forms of ancient writing. The word *hieroglyphic* comes from two Greek terms: *hieros*, meaning "sacred," and *glyphein*, meaning "to carve."

Egyptian hieroglyphic writing used two main kinds of symbols—ideograms and phonograms. Ideograms are pictures that represent a specific object or idea. A drawing of the sun, for instance, means "sun" or "day." Phonograms are "sound signs"—pictures that stand for specific sounds. Some phonograms represent a single sound. Others represent the combination of two or more sounds. By using ideograms and phonograms together, Egyptian writers could express many ideas in great detail.

For centuries, beginning around 3000 B.C., Egyptians mainly used hieroglyphics for religious inscriptions on monuments and temples.

▲ Ancient Egyptian hieroglyphic writing combined pictures that stood for sounds with pictures that stood for objects or ideas. These hieroglyphics from around 2052 B.C. come from Heracleopolis, the capital of Lower Egypt from 2185 to 2060 B.C.

They referred to this form of writing as "the words of God." Later, merchants and politicians relied on the system as well. Trained writers called scribes wrote the symbols on papyrus using ink or carved them on stones.

Hieroglyphic writing was very difficult to learn. At first the system had more than eight hundred different symbols. By 300 B.C. the number was up to more than six thousand. Scribes wrote in hieroglyphics from top to bottom. But hieroglyphic symbols could be written from left to right or right to left. Readers had to pay attention to the direction hieroglyphs faced to understand a message.

OTHER WAYS OF WRITING

The ancient Egyptians developed hieratic writing around the same time they developed the hieroglyphic system. Hieratic symbols often look like simplified versions of hieroglyphic images. The hieratic system also included fewer symbols than the hieroglyphic system. Archaeologists have found some samples of hieratic religious writing, but many of the documents they've discovered are personal letters or business records.

Scribes typically wrote with the hieratic system on papyrus, using sharpened reeds as pens and ink made from water and soot. Hieratic writing is a form of longhand, or cursive—the end of one letter usually connected to the letter that follows. A scribe using hieratic writing could work quickly, writing a line without lifting his pen.

Around 700 B.C., Egyptian scribes developed a form of writing known as demotic writing. Demotic writing looks much like a simplified form of hieratic writing. Scribes could write with this system even more quickly. Both systems were written from left to right and top to bottom. Scribes also used demotic for letter-writing and record-keeping.

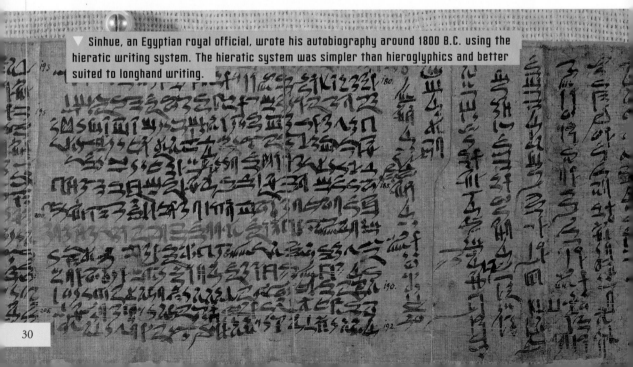

▼ Sinhue, an Egyptian royal official, wrote his autobiography around 1800 B.C. using the hieratic writing system. The hieratic system was simpler than hieroglyphics and better suited to longhand writing.

LIMESTONE SCRAP PAPER

etween 1550 and 1100 B.C., the ancient Egyptians buried their royalty in a special cemetery called the Valley of the Kings. Scribes, artists, painters, and other skilled craftspeople decorated the tombs of rulers buried in the cemetery. These craftspeople lived in a town near the Valley of the Kings called Deir el-Medina *(below)*.

An unusually large number of the men of Deir el-Medina were literate—around 40 percent at times. For scrap paper, the men used flakes of limestone called *ostraca (above)*. They made scratches on the stone with sharp tools. Deir el-Medina was buried under desert sands three thousand years ago. But archaeologists digging at the site have found thousands of ostraca containing notes, receipts for deliveries, and even love songs.

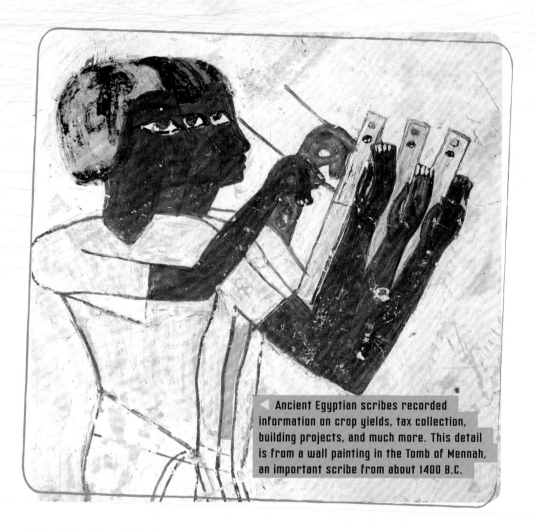

THE LIFE OF A SCRIBE

Writers were well respected in Egypt. Fewer than one in one hundred adults in ancient Egypt could read or write. One piece of ancient papyrus describes a father urging his child to become a scribe. "The profession of scribe is a princely profession," the man said. "His writing materials and his rolls of books bring pleasantness and riches."

Ancient Egyptian merchants, religious leaders, and government officials all depended on scribes. Scribes wrote down laws, maintained records, copied old documents, and helped explain religious rules. The life of a scribe was better than the life of a typical Egyptian. The Egyptian government required many citizens to work on dangerous projects such as building pyramids. But scribes worked in clean, safe conditions, usually in palaces.

The job was competitive. To become a scribe, a person had to know how to read, write, and do arithmetic. A scribe usually went to school and then served as an apprentice, working with experienced scribes for a period of years to perfect his skills. Egyptian scribes had to master hieroglyphic, hieratic, and demotic writing. In 332 B.C., the Greek army conquered Egypt. After this time, scribes had to learn Greek forms of writing as well, so they could work for their new rulers.

CHAPTER FOUR

ANCIENT INDIA

▲ The Indus River valley provided fertile ground for the earliest settlements in ancient India and Pakistan.

People in western India began settling into villages around 4000 B.C. Within one thousand years, one of the ancient world's greatest civilizations had emerged in this region. It covered an area of around 300,000 square miles (777,000 sq. km) in modern-day Pakistan and India. The civilization is called the Indus Valley Civilization because it developed in fertile areas along the Indus River.

About 1700 B.C., people began to leave the Indus valley. Experts believe that floods or changing river patterns may have caused the end of the Indus Valley Civilization. Two hundred years later, Aryans, a warlike people from central Asia, invaded India. They drove the earlier inhabitants southward. Aryan invaders spread throughout northern India and settled into villages.

The Aryans brought with them the Sanskrit language. For the next several hundred years, this language spread throughout ancient India. Indian writers used Sanskrit to write about religious rituals and to retell myths and legends.

SANSKRIT LIT

Many modern people would not think of literature as a form of technology. But throughout history, people have written or told stories as a way to spread religious and cultural teachings. Historians divide ancient Indian literature into three stages. The first, called the Vedic period, lasted from about 1400 to 500 B.C. During this time, priests known as Brahmans began to record prayers, religious songs, and instructions for other priests. The writings of the Brahmans make up four books called the Vedas. (*Veda* means "knowledge" in Sanskrit.) Historians refer to the early form of Sanskrit found in the books as Vedic Sanskrit.

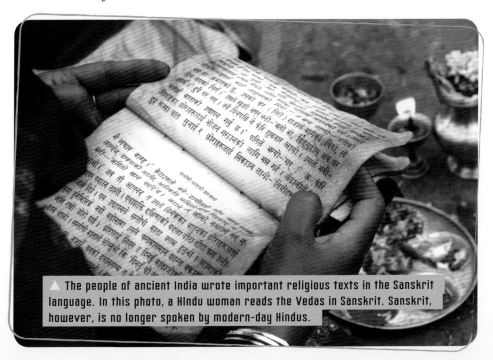

▲ The people of ancient India wrote important religious texts in the Sanskrit language. In this photo, a Hindu woman reads the Vedas in Sanskrit. Sanskrit, however, is no longer spoken by modern-day Hindus.

The earliest of the books, the *Rig-Veda*, dates to around 1400 B.C. The *Rig-Veda* contains more than one thousand religious hymns, or singable poems. Over the next several hundred years, Indian writers produced three other Vedas: the *Sama-Veda*, *Yajur-Veda*, and *Atharva-Veda*. These books also contained religious poems and mantras. Mantras are spiritual sayings that ancient Indians repeated as a form of prayer.

In most cases, historians are unsure of the names of specific people who worked on the Vedas. They believe countless religious leaders took part in writing down the books' hymns and mantras.

The second stage of ancient Indian literature is known as the epic period. The epic period covers the years around 500 B.C. It marks the writing of two famous Sanskrit epic poems, the *Ramayana* and the *Mahabharata*. An epic poem is a long story told through verse. The poems pass on moral lessons and encourage readers to follow the examples of their heroes.

Buildings at Angkor Wat, constructed in the early 1100s in modern-day Cambodia, are covered with reliefs illustrating the Sanskrit epic poems *Ramayana* and *Mahabharata*. This scene depicts a royal procession from the *Ramayana*.

> ## "As birds are made to fly and rivers to run, so the soul to follow duty."

—From the *Ramayana*, an ancient Indian epic poem, ca. 500 B.C.

The *Ramayana* tells the story of Rama, a prince who saves his wife from a powerful demon. The *Mahabharata* tells the story of a family divided by a war between two kingdoms. Both poems identify an author by name—the poet Valmiki in the *Ramayana* and the poet Vyasa in the *Mahabharata*. But many historians don't believe that either poem had a single author. Indian peoples probably told the epics orally well before 500 B.C., adding new parts over the years.

ANCIENT GRAMMAR

The third stage of ancient Indian literature is known as the classical period. The classical period lasted from about 500 B.C. to A.D. 1000.

THE TALE OF TEN PRINCES

In the sixth or seventh century the Indian writer Dandin authored a book called the *Dashakumaracharita*. Dandi's book describes the marriages and adventures of ten princes. Some scholars think of the *Dashakumaracharita* as one of the world's first novels.

Unlike the authors of earlier works such as the *Ramayana*, Dandin chose not to tell his story in verse (in the form of a poem). Instead, he wrote the *Dashakumaracharita* in the form of prose—a style of writing closer to spoken language. Prose works do not keep to a line-by-line structure like most poems. While many works of poetry feature rhyming lines or a steady rhythm, most prose works do not.

Historians associate the start of this period with the life of the writer Panini, who was most likely born in the 500s B.C. Panini wrote a guide to Sanskrit grammar that was used by later generations of Sanskrit writers and speakers.

A grammar system is a set of rules for using a language. It explains how nouns, pronouns, verbs, adverbs, and other parts of speech should be put together into proper sentences. The rules help writers and speakers use language clearly and without unnecessary or confusing words.

As with all languages, Sanskrit changed over time. The Sanskrit that people spoke at the end of the Vedic period would probably have sounded strange to people at the beginning of the classical period. Panini's guide, called *Ashtadhyayi*, provided almost four thousand rules for the Sanskrit language over eight chapters. The *Ashtadhyayi* helped people write a form of Sanskrit that they believed was correct and consistent with tradition.

Panini was not the first person to study grammar. He based his work on the teachings of earlier Indian scholars. But no one before Panini had put together a guide as detailed or thorough as the *Ashtadhyayi*.

ASHOKA SAYS

Around 324 B.C., a new empire took form in ancient India. Chandragupta Maurya, a leader descended from India's Aryan conquerors, united northern India under his rule. He created the Mauryan Empire, which controlled the north for about one hundred years. Chandragupta's grandson, the emperor Ashoka, ruled India from about 269 to 232 B.C. Ashoka developed one of the ancient world's earliest and best road-sign systems.

Road signs are an example of an important form of communication known as mass communication. They send messages to many people at the same time. Emperor Ashoka ordered that stone pillars be posted along the

Royal Road, a 1,700-mile-long (2,736 km) trade route that ran from the Middle Eastern city of Susa (in present-day Iran) to northern India. The huge pillars provided travelers with directions along the road. The pillars also featured advice from Ashoka. He urged travelers to obey laws and to be good citizens. One pillar reminds travelers that "it is good to give, but there is no gift, no service, like the gift of righteousness."

CHAPTER FIVE

ANCIENT CHINA

Chinese society emerged between 5000 and 3000 B.C. in the Yellow River valley of northern China. Early peoples settled into small farming villages that grew larger over time. The ancient Chinese made some of the most important contributions to communication technology. They invented paper and developed printing techniques.

For the most part, the Chinese developed their communication technology in isolation. China's people had limited contact with other ancient societies. So the Chinese came up with solutions to communication problems independently.

NO ALPHABET NEEDED

The earliest known examples of Chinese writing date to the eighteenth century B.C. Archaeologists have found symbols carved on pieces of bone and tortoiseshell. These early instances of writing were pictographic. The carvings feature drawings meant to represent different objects.

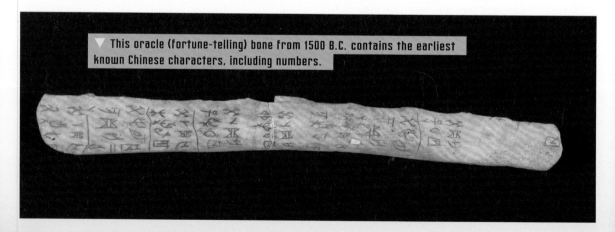

▼ This oracle (fortune-telling) bone from 1500 B.C. contains the earliest known Chinese characters, including numbers.

As the Chinese writing system evolved, Chinese writers used pictographs less often. But unlike the peoples of many other ancient societies, the Chinese did not create a shared alphabet. Instead, they developed a logographic system. In logographic writing, symbols stand for words or parts of words rather than the sounds used to make those words. By around 1400 B.C. the Chinese writing system included more than two thousand commonly used symbols.

TAPA BOOKS

The ancient Chinese wrote on many different materials before learning to produce paper. In fact, they were making books centuries before paper was invented. By around 3000 B.C. writers used a strong, flexible material called tapa. To make tapa, a person peeled the pale inner bark from a mulberry, fig, or laurel tree. He or she then dried and pounded the bark until it was smooth enough to write upon.

To put a book together, a person made holes in sheets of tapa and tied the sheets together with string. These books didn't last very long, however. The tapa pages tended to crack and rot. Books were also not common in ancient China. Tapa was expensive and only available in limited amounts.

The Chinese also wrote on pieces of silk, made from the cocoons of silkworms. But silk, like tapa, was expensive. Only the richest people could afford to use it for writing.

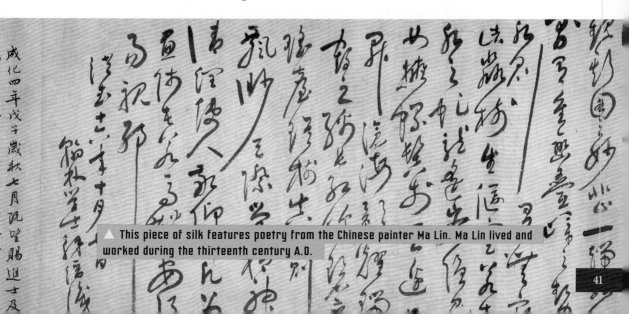

▲ This piece of silk features poetry from the Chinese painter Ma Lin. Ma Lin lived and worked during the thirteenth century A.D.

CHINESE INK

The Chinese made their first inks from berries, tree bark, and other natural substances. Many plants contain tannins. These chemicals can impart a pale yellow or light brown color to paper and other material. Early Chinese inkmakers used tannin from tea leaves and other local plants.

Historians believe a man named Tien-Tchen developed Chinese ink, also known as India ink, between 2600 and 2500 B.C. Chinese ink is one of the finest inks used for writing and illustration. It is velvety smooth and flows onto a writing surface in rich black lines. To create this type of ink, early Chinese inkmakers relied on carbon black, a sooty material produced by burning tar, pitch, or bone.

Unlike many other inks, Chinese ink was not kept in liquid form. Inkmakers mixed carbon black with glues or gums. They then molded the ink into cakes or sticks. The glue allowed the mixture to hold its shape. To write with Chinese ink, a person placed an ink stick in water before moving it across a surface.

▼ A traditional set of Chinese writing instruments includes *(from left to right)* an ink stick (in the shape of an animal), an ink slab for mixing the ink with water, and brushes for writing.

No one knows for sure why the same substance is known as both Chinese ink and India ink. People in ancient Greece, Rome, and the Middle East didn't know much about remote lands like India and China and may have considered them all to be the same.

FEAR OF BOOKS

Until the third century B.C., ancient China was made up of small warring states. During the third century, the state known as Qin conquered the states around it. By 221 B.C. the ruler Qin Shi Huangdi had unified all the rival states into a single powerful nation.

When Qin Shi Huangdi took power in 221 B.C., people in different parts of the huge country used different characters to stand for the same words. People in one area often couldn't understand the writing of people in another. Emperor Qin understood that a united people needed a shared writing system. He also wanted to make sure that everyone understood his orders. So he ordered everyone to use the same set of about three thousand pictograms. This same writing system is still in use in China more than two thousand years later.

▲ This is a statue of ancient Chinese emperor Qin Shi Huangdi, who ordered the Chinese people to use a shared writing system.

CONFUCIUS

The philosopher Kong Qui is one of China's most famous writers. Kong Qui lived from 551 to 479 B.C. Most modern people know him as Confucius *(below)*. This name is the Latin form of Kongfuzi, or K'ung-Fu-tzu, a Chinese phrase meaning "Great Master Kong."

Confucius spent his adult life first as a teacher and then as a government official. He encouraged people to live honest lives and to treat others in an ethical way. He believed that people learn best through public service and interaction with others.

During his lifetime, Confucius was not well known outside his province. But his followers wrote down his teachings in a book called *The Analects*. After Confucius's death in 479, his advice spread throughout ancient China. *The Analects* influenced Chinese thought for hundreds of years afterward.

Most of Confucius's thoughts were serious and practical. One teaching was, "To store up knowledge in silence, to remain forever hungry for learning, to teach others without tiring— all this comes to me naturally." Another was, "Set your heart upon the Way; rely upon moral power; follow goodness; enjoy the arts."

> **"I collected all the writings of the empire and got rid of those which were no use . . . Handsomely as I treated . . . the scholars, they are libeling [insulting] me, making out that I lack virtue."**

—Qin Shi Huangdi, Chinese emperor, on scholars who rebelled against book burning, 212 B.C.

In 213 B.C., Qin Shi Huangdi ordered that all books in China be burned, except those dealing with medicine, agriculture, the history of the Qin state, and a few other topics. He believed that books written before the new writing system was developed would hold back China's progress. Many people refused to comply with the order. A lot of old books survived, but at a great cost. Qin Shi Huangdi had scholars executed for owning and preserving the forbidden books.

REAL PAPER

The Han dynasty (family of rulers) led China after Qin Shi Huangdi's reign. They ruled from 206 B.C. to A.D. 200. This period was a time of great economic growth for China. It also produced one of our most basic communication tools—paper.

The difficulties that tapa posed as a writing surface frustrated Emperor Ho-ti, one of the Han rulers. In A.D. 104 he asked a member of the royal court named Ts'ai Lun to create an alternative. Ts'ai Lun experimented with different kinds of tree bark and natural fibers. By A.D. 105 he had developed a writing surface much like modern-day paper. Ts'ai Lun made his paper from mulberry tree bark and crushed bamboo. The material was strong but flexible and easier to produce than tapa.

Chinese papermakers usually soaked bark and bamboo in water until they became very soft and were almost ready to fall apart. Then they separated

the fibers by beating and stirring them in water. This process resulted in a thick, soupy mixture called pulp. Papermakers spread the pulp on a screen the desired size of the piece of paper. As the pulp dried, the fibers stuck together, forming a single sheet.

PRINTING

Printing is a technique for producing multiple identical copies of a document. In the second century A.D., around the same time Ts'ai Lun developed paper, Chinese clothmakers began printing pictures and designs on fabric. They used a technique called block printing.

Printmaking had been less practical in China and elsewhere before the second century. Papyrus was too fragile for printing. Parchment and vellum, made from animal skins, were too expensive. But the paper developed by Ts'ai Lun was just right—durable and affordable.

To make block prints, clothmakers carved raised words or designs on wooden blocks. The clothmakers put ink on the raised images and pressed the blocks onto sheets of fabric. Chinese printmakers soon used the same technique to transfer writing onto paper.

SPREADING THE WORD

Printing allowed people to copy books and other documents faster than ever before. Before the invention of printing, scribes sometimes had to write for months just to copy a single book by hand. Because the process was so time-consuming, few books were available.

When a product is scarce, it also is expensive. During much of ancient times, books were so costly that only kings, emperors, and other wealthy people could afford them. Printing made books less costly and thus available to more people.

Producing books by block printing was still expensive, however. Each page of a book required its own carved block. Once carved, the block could not be used to print anything else. In the eleventh century A.D. the Chinese improved printing even more with the invention of movable type. This consisted of small clay blocks, each stamped with one letter of the alphabet or another symbol. Since each letter was separate, the blocks could be arranged to form any word. Printers were able to use one set of blocks again and again.

▲ The *Diamond Sutra (above)* is the oldest known printed book. Chinese printmakers produced the book in A.D. 868.

CHAPTER SIX

THE ANCIENT AMERICAS

About thirty thousand years ago, a land bridge connected northeastern Asia and northwestern North America. Early peoples from Asia probably followed herds of animals across the bridge into Alaska. People then moved south through present-day Canada, onto the American Great Plains (the land west of the Mississippi River and east of the Rocky Mountains), and into present-day Mexico and Central America. The Paleo-Indians (ancient Native Americans) had reached the tip of South America by about 11,000 B.C.

Numerous separate cultures developed throughout the Americas. And like the Chinese, the early cultures of the Americas developed independently from those in Europe or the Middle East. The Paleo-Indians had no way to learn about the tools and techniques emerging in distant lands. Many Paleo-Indian groups relied upon the spoken word to share lessons and preserve their culture. Parents told their children legends about the start of the world or tales of great heroes. These stories moved across generations without tools other than the human voice, memory, and imagination. But the early peoples of North and South America also devised a wide variety of other communication technologies.

SHARED SYSTEMS

The beliefs and practices of Native American peoples were very different throughout the ancient Americas. So were their languages. Historians believe that Native Americans spoke as many as three hundred different languages north of Mexico alone. Some of these languages were similar, especially if the peoples who spoke them lived close to each other. But conversation among people of different tribes was often impossible.

This painting from 1846 shows Native Americans fishing for salmon at Kettle Falls on the Columbia River in the U.S. Pacific Northwest. They used many of the same fishing techniques as their ancestors, who traded with neighboring Native American groups using a shared language.

Sometimes multiple cultures shared a trade language—a language they all spoke when exchanging food or goods. This language was usually the native language of a group that lived in a high-trade area. The Chinook lived near the Columbia River in modern-day Oregon and Canada. The Chinook and several other groups used a waterfall in Chinook territory as a place of trade. Over time, the other groups came to use the Chinook language during trades.

Native Americans across the Great Plains spoke many different languages. Rather than establishing a shared verbal language, peoples such as the Cheyenne and the Comanche developed a system that let them pass on information without speaking. Plains Sign Language was based on gestures made with the hands.

Experts aren't sure when Native Americans began to use sign language. But the system became increasingly important in the A.D. 1500s. In that century, European settlers arrived in the Americas. The settlers introduced horses to the native peoples. Horses allowed the peoples of the Great Plains to travel long distances and interact more often.

Native Americans used Plains Sign Language into the 1800s. At this time, white settlers were pushing the peoples in and east of the Plains toward the west. The sign-language system continued to develop as new groups were forced to share the same areas.

▲ A Cheyenne man demonstrates sign language in the early twentieth century. Native peoples in the Americas relied on sign language to communicate across tribal cultures that did not share the same spoken language.

TOTEM POLES

Native American peoples of the northwestern United States and Canada created colorful carved wooden posts known as totem poles *(right)*. Totem poles featured pictographs representing animals, spirits, and people from a community. Totem poles served many purposes. Some were simply decorative posts that supported the roofs of houses. Some hollowed-out poles contained the remains of the deceased. But many totem poles included messages or even told stories.

Northwestern peoples placed "welcoming poles" at the edge of bodies of water to label their territories. They built memorial poles when a house changed owners, to identify old and new owners. If a notable individual let down his or her tribe, northwestern peoples carved his or her picture upside down on a "ridicule pole." Occasionally people also carved tall, detailed poles that told the legend of an entire family or community through pictographs. To read these legends, a person has to know the symbols and history of a Native American group extremely well.

MESOAMERICAN WRITERS

Researchers have found examples of early writing from several different cultures in present-day Mexico and Central America. Historians use the term *Mesoamerica* to describe this area and its cultures prior to the arrival of European explorers in the 1500s.

The Olmec people lived in parts of Mexico between 1200 and 400 B.C. Recent discoveries suggest that they may have been the first culture in the Americas to develop a writing system. In 2006 archaeologists studying the ancient Olmec site of San Lorenzo found a stone tablet dating from around 900 B.C. The tablet, called the Cascajal Block, displays twenty-eight distinct symbols and sixty-two symbols in total. It is the earliest known example of writing in either North or South America.

Before the discovery of the Cascajal Block, most historians believed that the Zapotec were the first society in the ancient Americas to write. Zapotec society emerged a few centuries after Olmec society in the area of southern Mexico known as Oaxaca. Archaeologists have found examples of

▼ Olmec peoples carved gigantic stone heads, like this one at San Lorenzo, Mexico, from about 1500 to 800 B.C. Archaeologists believe they have found evidence of Olmec writing at the site too.

picture writing on the remains of Zapotec monuments. The oldest known example of Zapotec writing comes from a stone known as Monument 3. The surface of Monument 3 shows a drawing of a dead or injured man. Two pictographs are drawn between the man's legs. The symbols most likely represent the man's name. Monument 3 dates from between 600 and 500 B.C.

MAYAN WRITING

The Maya emerged around 2500 B.C. They developed a powerful empire in modern-day southern Mexico, Guatemala, Belize, El Salvador, and Honduras. And sometime around 300 B.C. they also developed one of the ancient America's most advanced writing systems.

Mayan writing was similar to Egyptian hieroglyphic writing in many respects. The writing system consists of more than seven hundred pictographs including faces, animals, and other objects. Each symbol carries one or more meanings. Mayan writers could combine pictographs to form words or ideas. They drew the images inside small squares and arranged the squares into columns. Mayan writing moves from left to right and top to bottom.

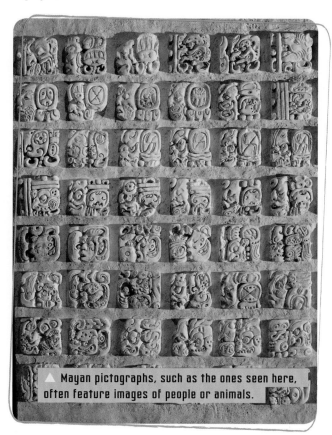

▲ Mayan pictographs, such as the ones seen here, often feature images of people or animals.

The Maya wrote books, painted inscriptions on pottery and walls, and carved words into stone monuments. Archaeologists have found many inscriptions on stelae, rectangular slabs of stone set upright like signs. Although archaeologists have deciphered many Mayan symbols, understanding whole phrases or stories is very difficult. The same symbol can represent several different sounds and ideas.

The ancient Maya wrote on long sheets of bark from fig trees that grows in the rain forest. Some sheets are more than 20 feet (6 m) long. Mayan writers covered the sheets with a white paint made from powdered limestone, water, and other materials. Priests and scribes wrote glyphs on the sheets with black ink made from soot. They folded each sheet into pleats, much like the folds in an accordion, to make a kind of book called a codex. Codices contained calendars, astronomical tables, and information about religious ceremonies.

▲ This Mayan codex from the fifteenth century A.D. depicts Quetzalcoatl, the Mayan god of knowledge and agriculture. Mayan artists often illustrated Quetzalcoatl as a feathered serpent.

JUST A COINCIDENCE?

Could the ancient Egyptians have somehow met the Maya and taught them to use hieroglyphic writing? Throughout the last century, a few historians have suggested that peoples from ancient Africa traveled across the Atlantic Ocean to Mesoamerica. The historians argue that by the first century A.D., Egyptian boats were sturdy enough to make the full voyage. They note similarities between African and Mesoamerican languages. They point out that multiple Mesoamerican cultures built pyramidlike structures.

Most historians reject the idea that ancient Egyptians visited the ancient Americas. No archaeologist has found physical evidence of an Egyptian visit. The Maya probably devised picture writing without assistance. The Egyptians and the Maya both needed a way to record events. Both realized that the picture-writing system suited their needs.

LIBRARIES

Archaeologists believe that the Maya stored codices in big libraries. Literate Maya were typically priests or rulers, and the libraries were most likely collected within large temples. Many of the books rotted over time in the hot, wet rain forest climate. However, a small number survived for centuries.

In 1519 Spanish explorers landed in Mexico. They discovered ancient books written by the Maya. Spanish priests tried to convert the descendents of the Maya to Christianity. On July 12, 1562, a group of Spanish priests punished people who would not convert by burning a large collection of Mayan religious artifacts, including forty ancient books. With the books burned, modern archaeologists have few clues to help them understand ancient Mayan civilization or to decipher the Mayan writing system. Only three books and bits of a fourth have survived to modern times.

> "These people . . . used certain characters or letters, with which they wrote in their books about the antiquities [ancient times] and their sciences . . . We found a great number of books in these letters, and, since they contained nothing but superstitions and falsehoods . . . we burned them all, which they took most grievously, and gave them great pain."

—Diego de Landa, Spanish missionary, on the burning of Mayan books, 1566

PAINTED WALLS

In addition to writing, the Maya painted beautiful pictures on pottery and walls of temples. In the 1940s archaeologists discovered the remains of an ancient Mayan settlement in southern Mexico. One building had walls covered with colorful paintings showing warfare and warriors taking and killing prisoners. The archaeologists named the settlement Bonampak, a Mayan word meaning "painted wall."

The Bonampak murals were a sensation. Until then, experts had assumed that the Maya were a peace-loving people who seldom or never waged war. The murals helped archaeologists realize that warfare was an important part of Mayan civilization.

THE QUIPU

The Inca lived throughout much of South America in the 1400s and 1500s. Their empire included parts of present-day Colombia, Ecuador, Peru, Chile, Bolivia, and Argentina. To keep track of crops and taxes, the Inca relied on devices called quipus. Quipus were made of threads of cotton or animal

hair. On most quipus, multiple threads hung from one long rope. Sometimes smaller threads hung from the main threads. A single quipu could have hundreds of threads or only a few.

Historians believe that the Incan record-keepers known as *Quipucamayocs* developed the quipu. To use a quipu, a Quipucamayoc tied knots on the strings. Knots stood for different numerical amounts, usually in amounts of ten. The Inca occasionally used color-coded strings in addition to recording information with knots. Government officials and village leaders were responsible for storing quipus.

As with Mayan codices, Spanish explorers destroyed many Incan quipus in the 1500s. The Spanish feared that the Inca were using quipus to spread dangerous messages. But modern-day researchers have been able to find and preserve several hundred ancient quipus.

CHAPTER SEVEN

ANCIENT GREECE

▲ The Greeks performed famous comedies and dramas in the Theater of Herodes Atticus. The theater, which sits on the Acropolis in Athens, Greece, was built in A.D 160.

Ancient Greece was a great center of art and learning. The Greeks wrote famous plays, histories, poems, and speeches that modern people still read and enjoy. Few ancient people actually read these works. Instead, the Greeks spread poems and stories through speech. Actors and orators (public speakers) memorized the famous works and recited them to audiences. The Greeks passed some stories and poems down through generations without writing them down for hundreds of years. Most ancient Greeks had little need for written communication anyway. Writing was important mainly for government officials, who kept track of laws and taxes, and for merchants, who kept business records.

As ancient Greece became more involved with other countries, written communication became more important. The Greek military leader Alexander the Great, who lived from 356 to 323 B.C., conquered many surrounding countries, including Egypt. Alexander and his assistants needed to keep track of current events in these countries, where people spoke many different languages. Written records were the best way to deal with the flood of new information.

BORROWING FROM THE PHOENICIANS

For years, Greek merchants regularly traded with the Phoenicians. So the ancient Greeks became quite familiar with the Phoenician alphabet. Around 800 B.C., the Greeks began to use it to write their own language. They borrowed nineteen of the Phoenicians' twenty-two letters. They also added a few new letters, including *phi* (Φ) and *psi* (Ψ), to represent sounds missing from the Phoenician alphabet.

▲ The ancient Greeks' writing system *(left)* was patterned on that of the Phoenicians *(right)*.

Although the Greeks kept the Phoenician symbols, they changed many pronunciations. The Phoenician symbol *aleph* (A or α) was renamed "alpha." It became the first letter of the Greek alphabet. The symbol *beth* (B or β) was changed to "beta." It became the second letter.

At first the Greeks wrote like the Phoenicians, from right to left and then left to right. This method was known as *boustrophedon*, which means "like an ox turning." It referred to the way farmers plowed a field with oxen, moving one way down a row, then turning and plowing the next row in the opposite direction. Greek writers also sometimes flipped letters around so they faced in the opposite direction. Around 500 B.C., the Greeks adopted a standard writing direction: left to right. They adopted a standard twenty-four-letter alphabet around 400 B.C.

BOOKS WITHOUT PAGES

The ancient Greeks adopted the practice of making paper from papyrus, learning the technique from the people of ancient Egypt. Greek writers mention papyrus as early as the sixth century B.C. More than thirty thousand

THE ANCIENT TELEGRAPH

Around 500 B.C., the Greeks designed a system to quickly send messages from one city to another. The system is known in modern times as a visual telegraph. The Greeks built a series of towers between major cities. Each tower could be easily seen from the tower nearest to it. Holes at the tops of the towers represented letters in the Greek alphabet. By lighting fires in the right holes, Greeks could send simple messages, such as "danger."

Researchers have been fortunate to find thousands of preserved Greek scrolls. This papyrus scroll from the first century B.C. features thoughts from the Greek scholar Didymus Chalcenterus.

Greek papyrus scrolls have survived to modern times. The oldest preserved scrolls date to the fourth century B.C.

The Greeks were very practical bookmakers—they wanted to fit as much information as possible on each scroll. Whereas the Egyptians often wrote in fancy lettering that took up lots of room, the Greeks wrote in small letters. They wrote in columns about 3 inches (8 cm) wide, with thin spaces between columns and margins on each side of the page. The Egyptians sometimes added drawings as decorations on their scrolls. But the Greeks included only drawings that communicated information— such as a diagram that showed how a machine worked.

The Greeks kept scrolls small enough for readers to hold them comfortably. Greek scrolls did not exceed 35 feet (11 m) in length. Rolled up, a

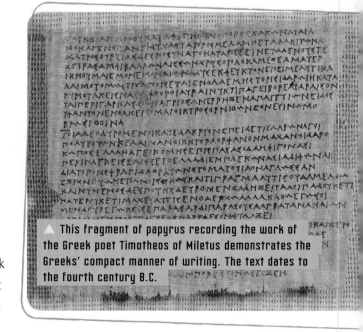

This fragment of papyrus recording the work of the Greek poet Timotheos of Miletus demonstrates the Greeks' compact manner of writing. The text dates to the fourth century B.C.

typical scroll measured between 1 and 1.5 inches (2.5 to 4 cm) in diameter. Scrolls were 9 or 10 inches (23 or 25 cm) high. Readers didn't turn pages, they just unrolled the scroll—usually unrolling with the right hand while rewinding with the left hand. Some scrolls wrapped around a wooden roller. Knobs on the roller made it easier to neatly wind the scrolls.

FROM EPIC POEMS TO PROSE

Many well-known and widely-used forms of literature have roots in ancient Greece. In the 700s B.C. the poet Homer wrote two famous epic poems, the *Iliad* and the *Odyssey*. The *Iliad* tells the legend of the Trojan War, which supposedly took place in the twelfth or thirteenth century B.C. The *Odyssey* tells the story of Odysseus, a hero of the Trojan War who struggles to return home to his wife. Homer based his poems on stories that the Greeks had passed down across centuries of oral storytelling.

During the 400s B.C. drama flourished in Greece. Greek people flocked to see actors perform the works of playwrights such as Sophocles. Sophocles' plays often ended tragically and featured powerful moral lessons. His work *Oedipus Rex* tells the story of a ruler, Oedipus, who seeks the murderer of a man whom Oedipus himself unknowingly killed. Unlike most modern playwrights, Sophocles and his fellow writers composed their works in verse rather than prose.

▲ This is a marble statue of Sophocles. The playwright lived from 496 to 406 B.C. Sophocles wrote many famous Greek plays that are still performed in modern times.

> "For look you—whosoe'er [whosoever]
> did slay the king/
> Me too belike may smite [strike] with my slaught'rous
> [slaughtering] hand./
> Therefore, avenging him, myself I aid."

—Sophocles, Greek playwright, from *Oedipus Rex*, 420s B.C.

Around 450 B.C., another new form emerged: rhetoric, the art of effective speaking. A group of philosophers known as Sophists worked to determine the best ways to write and present arguments. As a result of their studies, public speaking grew in popularity across Greece. Spoken prose became an increasingly common way to present ideas among politicians and thinkers.

WHAT A LIBRARY!

Upon conquering Egypt in 332 B.C., Alexander the Great founded the city of Alexandria on Egypt's northern coast. Alexandria became home to the most famous library in the ancient world.

Ptolemy Soter, one of Alexander's generals, ruled Egypt from 323 to 285 B.C. Ptolemy and his adviser Demetrius of Phaleron began to build a great library for the scholars of Alexandria. Ptolemy's son, Ptolemy II, continued the project after his father's death. Greeks before Ptolemy had built other libraries, such as the first public library in the city of Athens. But the library of Alexandria was larger than any that had come before it.

The most famous writers and scholars of the day ran the library. They worked to collect the best Greek literature, as well as knowledge from the rest of the world, in one place. Over the years, the library of Alexandria gained more and more books—probably between one hundred thousand

and seven hundred thousand—including the largest known collection of medical books in the ancient world.

STUFF FROM PERGAMUM

Books became so important in ancient Greece that two rulers, Ptolemy V and Eumenes II, almost went to war over them. According to legend, Ptolemy V wanted the library at Alexandria to remain the largest

▲ The ruins of the great library of Alexandria, built in the 200s B.C., still stand in Egypt.

in the world. Eumenes founded his own library, located at Pergamum in modern-day Turkey. Eumenes wanted to have the world's largest collection of books.

Worried that Eumenes was getting ahead, Ptolemy banned the shipment of papyrus from Egypt to Pergamum. Eumenes needed a new substance for recording words on paper. Around 190 B.C., someone in his kingdom developed parchment. Parchment is a heavy, paperlike material made from the skins of sheep or lambs. In Latin and Greek, *parchment* means "stuff from Pergamum."

Other ancient people had written on animal skins before the people of Pergamum developed parchment. Records show that the Egyptians used leather as a writing surface in 2450 B.C. Scribes in ancient Mesopotamia may have done so as well. But leather, made by a different process than parchment, was not very good for writing. It was dark and rotted easily. Parchment was different. It was light in color, flexible, and long-lasting.

▲ The people of Pergamum (in modern-day Turkey) turned to parchment when papyrus became scarce. This parchment document from the eighth century features segments of the Gospel of Saint Luke, written in Greek.

To produce parchment, workers first removed all the hair and flesh from a dead animal's hide. Then they stretched the skin tightly in wooden frames. Workers treated the skin on both sides with chalk to make it brighter. Lastly, they rubbed the skin with pumice, a fine volcanic powder that made it silky smooth.

ONE THING LEADS TO ANOTHER

The development of parchment led, in the second century B.C., to the creation of modern-style books. The Greeks used papyrus to make books on scrolls. But they used parchment for books bound together along the side, like modern books.

THE FIRST MARATHON

In the ancient world, runners were the fastest way of sending messages from one place to another. Runners carried written messages for military leaders, kings, government officials, and traders. Sometimes runners also memorized long spoken messages. Runners often had to swim rivers and climb hills and mountains.

Greek legend tells of the most famous message ever delivered by foot. It was sent during the Persian Wars (499–449 B.C.). A Persian army landed at the Greek city of Marathon, about 25 miles (40 km) north of Athens. A small Greek force from Athens defeated the larger Persian army. The Greeks wanted to get news of the victory to Athens as quickly as possible.

According to the legend, the Greek commanders turned to their fastest runner, who had just returned from a 150-mile (241 km) trip to the city-state of Sparta. He took the assignment nonetheless, reached Athens, announced the Greek victory, and dropped dead of exhaustion. The modern marathon, which is 26 miles (42 km), 385 yards (352 m) long, is named in honor of his remarkable run.

Parchment was ideal for making bound books. The fibers of a papyrus plant lined up in such a way that it was difficult to write on both sides. But a scribe could use both sides of a parchment sheet for writing. So one sheet of parchment could hold twice as much information as a sheet of papyrus of the same size.

Parchment was also more flexible than papyrus. Sheets of parchment could be folded into individual pages. One fold in a sheet made a folio of two pages. Two folds made a quarto of four pages. Three folds made an octavo of eight pages. Bookmakers cut folded sheets and sewed them together to form a book that opened page by page. Bound books were much easier to read than

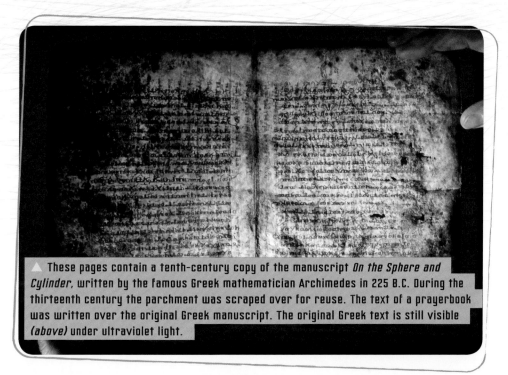

▲ These pages contain a tenth-century copy of the manuscript *On the Sphere and Cylinder*, written by the famous Greek mathematician Archimedes in 225 B.C. During the thirteenth century the parchment was scraped over for reuse. The text of a prayerbook was written over the original Greek manuscript. The original Greek text is still visible *(above)* under ultraviolet light.

scrolls. A person could open a bound book instantly to any page without having to unroll foot after foot of papyrus.

People often adopt new technology slowly—even if new technologies, such as parchment and bound books, are superior to old technologies. Even after the introduction of parchment, people still used papyrus scrolls. Parchment did not become the ancient world's main writing material until the fourth century A.D. And some ancient peoples continued to use papyrus scrolls for official government documents until the A.D. 900s.

CHAPTER EIGHT

ANCIENT ROME

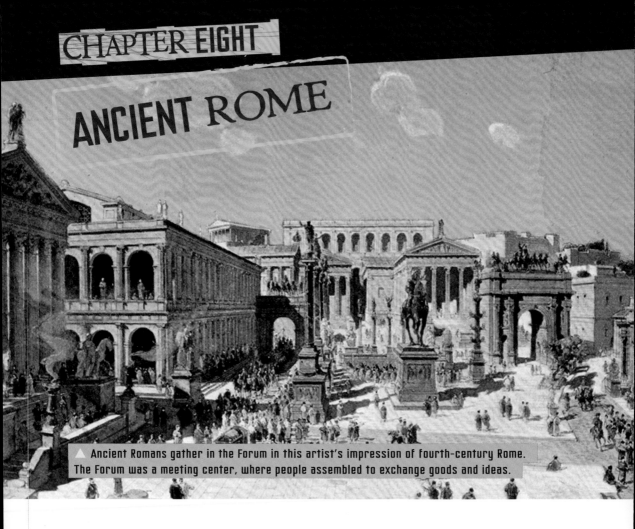

▲ Ancient Romans gather in the Forum in this artist's impression of fourth-century Rome. The Forum was a meeting center, where people assembled to exchange goods and ideas.

The empire of Rome began in present-day Italy. An ancient people called the Latins formed villages in central Italy around 750 B.C. One village grew into the city of Rome. The Romans overtook other groups in Italy and later throughout much of Europe. The ancient Romans made many advances in communication technology. Some of this technology spread to the cities and states that Rome conquered between the first and fifth centuries A.D.

Some of ancient Rome's most important contributions were Latin, the language of ancient Rome, and the Roman manner of writing.

MENSIS MENSIS MENSIS
OCTOBER NOVEMBER DECEMB
DIES·XXXI DIES·XXX DIES·XXXI
NONAE NON·QVINT NONQVINT
SEPTIMAN DIES·HOR·VIIIS DIES·HOR·VIIII
DIES NOX·HOR·XIIIS NOX·HOR·XV
HOR·X S= SOL SOI·SAGITT
NOX SCORPIONE TVTEL·VESTÆ
HOR·XIIIS TVTELA HEMPS·NITIV
DEANAE SIVE·TROPAE

▲ This ancient Roman calendar illustrates the Roman alphabet's close resemblance to the modern English alphabet.

The first traces of Latin appear in inscriptions dating from the sixth century B.C. The Romans based the Latin alphabet on the writing of the Etruscans, who ruled northern Italy from the eighth to the fifth century B.C. The Etruscans had modeled their alphabet after the Greek alphabet. The Latin alphabet was a lot like our English alphabet, except it had only twenty-three letters. The missing letters where *J*, *U*, and *W*.

Early Roman peoples used a few different forms of Latin. Historians divide these forms into three categories: early or preliterary (not written) Latin, Classical (written) Latin, and Vulgar (spoken and informal) Latin.

THE LATIN OF THE PEOPLE

The term *Vulgar Latin* comes from the ancient Romans themselves. *Vulgar Latin* refers to the many varieties of Latin used by people not trained in Classical Latin. These people were usually members of the middle and lower classes. Many of these peoples spoke forms of Latin that had elements of earlier ancient languages.

Researchers have learned about Vulgar Latin from a variety of sources. Not many written works of the Roman Empire feature the language, but a few plays featuring lower-class characters contain examples of Vulgar Latin. Some Classical Latin texts also mention Vulgar Latin as an example of how *not* to write. Archaeologists have found Vulgar Latin graffiti carved on the walls of Roman ruins, too.

Many historians believe that Vulgar Latin became part of modern-day Italian and French. Scholars who study these modern languages have noticed that they have features found in Latin but which Classical Latin writers avoided.

ROMAN CURSIVE

Roman scribes began to use cursive writing around the first century A.D. At first, Roman cursive was similar to the style of writing seen on Greek papyruses. Scribes sometimes connected words and characters with line strokes called ligatures. But the use of ligatures was not consistent from scribe to scribe.

Historians refer to the Romans' early style of longhand writing as Old Roman Cursive. The Romans used this form of writing for about three hundred years. In the A.D. 300s the style evolved into a new form of writing known as New Roman Cursive. The characters in Old Roman Cursive looked similar to modern capital letters. Characters in New Roman Cursive looked more like modern lowercase letters. This form of writing gradually developed into modern cursive.

LITTLE FEET

Take a close look at the letters on the opposite page. Do you notice the little "feet" on the bottom, top, and sides of some of the letters? These feet are actually called serifs.

Serifs make it easier to read lines of type on a page. The small feet lead our eyes from one letter to the next. Letters without serifs are called sans serif (*sans* means "without"). Historians aren't sure who developed writing with serifs or at what time. But many believe the invention of serifs took place during the age of the Roman Empire. Inscriptions on ancient Roman buildings display the earliest known examples of letters with serifs.

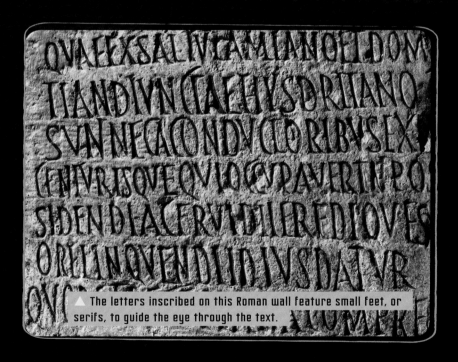

▲ The letters inscribed on this Roman wall feature small feet, or serifs, to guide the eye through the text.

One big difference between ancient Roman writing and our own is that the Romans rarely used commas or other punctuation. Roman scribes also used proper capital letters infrequently, usually just in headings.

BARK AND BEESWAX

Papyrus was scarce in parts of the Roman Empire, including northern Italy. So the Romans sometimes wrote on tree bark instead. In fact, the Latin word for book is *liber*, which means "bark." The Romans also wrote on very thin sheets of wood peeled from trees. Each sheet was called a *leaf*, a word we still use to mean a page in a book. Bark and wood dried out and rotted very quickly, however. The Romans mainly used these materials for letters and lists—items that didn't have to last long.

For records that had to last, the ancient Romans sometimes wrote on wax tablets. Tabletmakers filled wooden frames with beeswax. Writers used a pointed wooden stick called a stylus to scratch letters and numbers in

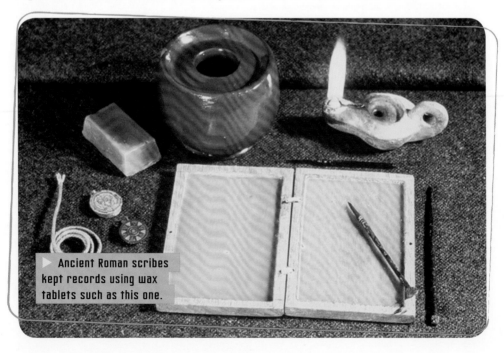

▶ Ancient Roman scribes kept records using wax tablets such as this one.

the wax. Wax tablets had holes in the edges so that several could be bound together with rings, like those used in modern loose-leaf binders. When the tablets were closed, the frames' raised edges protected the wax from damage.

GAIUS'S GIFT

Some ancient Romans considered books to be a form of treasure. Soldiers occasionally brought books home from countries they had defeated in battle. A Roman general named Lucius Licinius Lucullus built a huge home library of books he had taken from conquered lands. His library became a gathering place and a study for famous Roman and Greek writers such as Cicero, Cato, and Plutarch.

A soldier and historian named Gaius Asinius Pollio constructed Rome's first public library around 40 B.C. The space contained thousands of Roman and Greek books. Pollio also supported Roman writers of his time. He held events at which they could read aloud from their works.

Roman politicians eventually built many other public libraries. The buildings were often gifts from Roman leadership to cities and towns, a way to help keep citizens loyal to the emperor.

HUMAN PRINTING PRESSES

The printing techniques of ancient Rome were less advanced than those of ancient China. Books had to be copied by hand. Over time, Roman book publishers realized that it was very inefficient for one person to copy one book. So publishers hired people called readers and copyists.

To create multiple copies of books, a reader would slowly read a book to a room full of as many as thirty copyists. The copyists would write each word, making many copies of a book at the same time. This method made books cheaper to produce. As books became less expensive, more middle-class people could buy them.

FIRST DAILY NEWSPAPER

The world's first daily newspaper was probably ancient Rome's *Acta Diurna* (Daily Events). Roman leader Julius Caesar started *Acta Diurna* in 59 B.C. as a way to keep citizens informed of government decrees, new laws, and important events. But the newspaper also included human-interest items such as notices of births and deaths.

A group of scribes wrote copies of *Acta Diurna* by hand each day. Government workers posted copies of the paper in public places so that many people could read them.

TIME SAVERS

Abbreviations and acronyms make written communication simpler. When addressing a letter, for instance, it is easier to write the abbreviation *MN* than the full word *Minnesota*. The acronym *CJHS* is easier to write than *Central Junior High School*.

The ancient Romans developed hundreds of abbreviations and acronyms. *SPQR*, for example, was short for *Senatus Populusque Romanus* ("the senate and the Roman people"). The Romans used this abbreviation when referring to their government. *IMP* stood for *imperator*, the leader of the Roman army. Archaeologists have found Roman abbreviations on the surfaces of ancient coins and buildings.

"NEITHER SNOW, NOR RAIN, NOR HEAT..."

Many ancient civilizations developed postal systems for sending messages quickly over long distances. Rulers needed these systems to keep in touch with all parts of their empires.

Around 27 B.C., the Roman emperor Augustus Caesar developed the most advanced postal system in the ancient world. Roman couriers rode horses along Rome's paved roads. They rested or passed their messages along at relay stations called post houses. Post houses were separated by a distance that a courier could travel before tiring. At each relay station the courier passed his message to a fresh runner or exchanged his tired horse for a new one. In this way, messages always traveled at top speed.

At first the Romans used their postal system mainly for government business. Around A.D. 200, the Roman postal system began carrying private messages too.

AFTER THE ANCIENTS

Ancient societies rose and fell. Often groups grew politically or economically weak, and stronger groups conquered them. But even after a civilization died out, its technology often remained. Conquering groups built on the knowledge of conquered peoples to further develop technology.

This wasn't always the case, however. After the Roman Empire fell to invaders in A.D. 476, Europe entered a period called the Middle Ages (about 500 to 1500). The early Middle Ages are sometimes called the Dark Ages, because art, culture, and learning did not flourish in Europe during these years. Few people in Europe went to school. Few craftspeople knew about or improved upon ancient technology.

PAPERMAKING SPREADS

Some communication technology continued to spread during the Middle Ages. Peoples outside China were beginning to learn about the Chinese method of making paper. Papermaking reached the areas of modern-day Korea and Japan in the A.D. 600s. In A.D. 751 a Chinese army attacked Samarkand, a territory in modern-day Uzbekistan. A Middle Eastern people called the Moors controlled Samarkand. The Moors defeated the Chinese and took many prisoners. Among the prisoners were papermakers. The Chinese papermakers showed the Moors their technology.

The Moors set up paper mills in Baghdad, part of modern-day Iraq, around 795. Papermaking technology then spread to Spain, which the Moors also controlled. Between 1095 and 1291, Christian armies from Europe attacked Moorish lands in the Middle East during religious wars called the Crusades. During this time European Christians also discovered Chinese papermaking techniques.

A UNIVERSAL LANGUAGE

Latin remained in use after the fall of the Roman Empire. It became the "universal language" of Europe, which scholars learned in addition to their native languages. Using Latin, scientists and scholars communicated with educated people from other countries. Diplomats and government officials used it to carry out negotiations with foreign leaders.

In the 1300s Europeans took a renewed interest in learning, literature, art, and technology. Europe entered a period of creative outpouring called the Renaissance (1300s–1600). The name *Renaissance* means "rebirth." Renaissance writers used Latin for almost

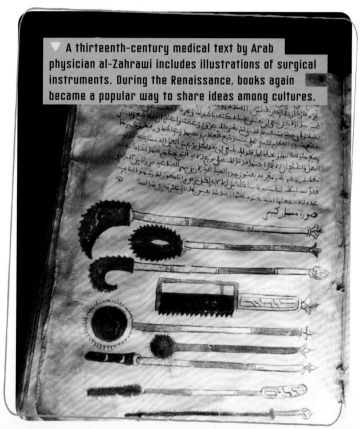

A thirteenth-century medical text by Arab physician al-Zahrawi includes illustrations of surgical instruments. During the Renaissance, books again became a popular way to share ideas among cultures.

all their works. Latin remained the universal language until the eighteenth century, when diplomats and scholars began to use French for the same purposes.

A NEW WAY TO PRINT

Johannes Gutenberg was a German inventor who lived from around 1400 to 1468. Gutenberg improved movable type and invented the modern printing press. By Gutenberg's time the Chinese no longer widely used movable type for printing. The Chinese language included so many characters that the method was difficult and time-consuming. But the method was well-suited to printing works in Latin.

Gutenberg's printing press used letters on equal-sized metal bodies that could be evenly arranged, locked in place, easily removed, and reused. No earlier printing press worked with the speed and efficiency of the one Gutenberg developed. In 1455 Gutenberg printed his first book, a Latin version of the Bible. Gutenberg's model for printing spread throughout Europe after his lifetime. His printing press made written works cheaper to produce and accessible to greater numbers of people.

THE ROSETTA STONE

The French emperor Napoleon invaded Egypt in 1798. In 1799 French soldiers at the Egyptian village of Rashid, or Rosetta, discovered a stone plaque inscribed with three distinct forms of writing. The soldiers knew that the stone was an important find and shipped it to their base in Cairo, Egypt. The French made copies of the stone and sent them to scholars throughout Europe.

The Rosetta stone weighed more than 1,650 pounds (750 kg). To scholars, it was worth its weight in gold. The stone featured a passage written (from top to bottom) in hieroglyphics, demotic writing, and Greek. Scholars quickly translated the Greek and found the words to be a decree issued by Egyptian ruler Ptolemy V in 196 B.C.

The stone included Greek because the Greeks ruled Egypt at the time of the writing. Scholars realized that the other kinds of writing repeated the same decree. They began comparing Greek words with the hieroglyphics at the top of the stone. They found hieroglyphic symbols for Greek names such as Ptolemy and gradually learned how to translate hieroglyphics into Greek. Knowing the Greek meanings of many hieroglyphics allowed scholars to translate the symbols into their own languages as well.

Deciphering the Rosetta stone took years of effort. A French expert, Jean-François Champollion, completed the work in 1822. Archaeologists used their new knowledge to translate hieroglyphic inscriptions on ancient Egyptian tombs and to learn more about ancient Egyptian civilization.

► The Rosetta stone of ancient Egypt presents a message from Egyptian ruler Ptolemy V in hieroglyphic *(top)*, demotic *(middle)*, and Greek *(bottom)* writing.

A SYSTEM FROM SCRATCH

Most writing systems developed slowly, with changes and additions from numerous people. But a single person named Sequoyah created a syllabary for North America's Cherokee people over about twelve years. For most of their history, the Cherokee had no written language. Sequoyah worked as a silversmith and regularly traded with white settlers. The settlers' written record-keeping methods impressed Sequoyah. Sequoyah began work on a Cherokee-language writing system around 1809.

Sequoyah struggled at first. In his earliest attempts, he tried designing symbols that matched up with whole words. Later, he designed symbols that

stood for syllables instead. By 1821 Sequoyah had produced a complete, eighty-six-word syllabary. He based some of the symbols on English letters, but his symbols represented different sounds.

Sequoyah's syllabary excited Cherokee leaders. The Cherokee Nation officially adopted the system in 1825.

◄ In 1821 a Cherokee man named Sequoyah created a syllabary based on all the sounds of the Cherokee language. Sequoyah's syllabary allowed the Cherokee to use written communication for the first time in their history.

THE NEW HIEROGLYPHICS

Hieroglyphic writing has not completely died out. Modern people rely on pictographs every day. Pictographs point the way to public restrooms, telephones, emergency exits, and baggage-claim areas in airports. A picture of a cigarette with a slash through it means that smoking is prohibited in the area. A road sign with a curvy line means that the road turns ahead.

Advances in transportation throughout the twentieth century made it easier for people to travel to foreign countries. In the 1970s the U.S. Department of Transportation made a list of fifty pictograms for airports and other places that foreign travelers use. Pictographs provide information to people who can't read writing in an area's native language. And in many cases, pictographic writing is simply more efficient than the written word. Most people understand the meaning of the signs designating men's and women's restrooms in an instant.

Some language experts have suggested that modern pictographs could lead to a new writing system that everyone in the world could understand. The system would use symbols that are not based in any one language. But other experts believe that such a system could never express the wide range of ideas put forth by a regular written language.

OUTER SPACE PICTOGRAPHS

In 1972 the United States space program launched *Pioneer 10*, a probe designed to study Jupiter and Saturn and continue on into deep space. The scientists realized that someday an extraterrestrial civilization might find *Pioneer 10*. They attached a message to a plaque on the probe's antenna. The scientists knew that beings from another planet would not understand any language used on Earth. So the message consisted of pictures and symbols.

The *Pioneer 10* plaque shows what male and female humans look like. The male figure's hand is raised in a gesture of goodwill. The plaque also indicates the size of an average human. It includes a silhouette of the *Pioneer 10*.

The craft's antenna is placed next to the human figures. By measuring the antenna's height, alien beings would be able to figure out human proportions.

Circles at the bottom of the plaque show that *Pioneer 10* was launched by people living on the third planet from the sun—Earth—and show Earth's size compared to the sun. Crossed lines show the sun's position in our galaxy, the Milky Way. Two circles at the upper left corner of the plaque show scientific information about hydrogen, the most common chemical element in the universe.

THEN AND NOW

Many of the twenty-first century's most popular communication technologies might seem to have little in common with those of the ancient world. With smartphones and laptops, people can send and receive information faster than ever before and across greater distances. The Internet, a communications network connecting computers throughout the planet, stores information about a nearly limitless array of subjects. Never before have so many people had access to so much information or so may ways to share it. But all modern communication techniques and tools owe something to the inventions of the past.

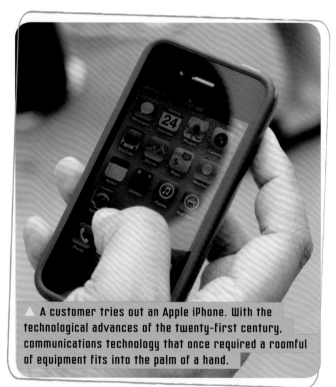

▲ A customer tries out an Apple iPhone. With the technological advances of the twenty-first century, communications technology that once required a roomful of equipment fits into the palm of a hand.

The basics of human communication have remained the same since ancient times. Most people in Europe and the Americas still rely on writing systems that evolved from those of the Romans, who borrowed from the Greeks, who borrowed from the Phoenicians. Despite the growth of electronic communication, many people still record information on paper made from wood pulp throughout their daily lives. And people continue to express their values and teach lessons through literature. Although the peoples of the ancient world could not have predicted the ways modern people would communicate, many aspects of their cultures can still be seen in our own.

TIMELINE

CA. 30,000 B.C.	Ancient people paint in caves for the first time.
CA. 10,000 B.C.	Ancient people begin to form permanent villages.
3000s B.C.	Mesopotamian writers begin scratching pictographic records on clay tablets.
3000s B.C.	Chinese writers develop tapa for use as a writing surface.
CA. 3100 B.C.	Egyptian peoples learn how to make paper from papyrus.
3000s B.C.	Egyptian peoples begin to write with hieroglyphics.
CA. 2800 B.C.	Middle Eastern peoples begin to use pictures to stand for specific sounds.
2500s B.C.	Tien-Tchen develops Chinese ink.
2000s B.C.	Mesopotamian peoples begin sharing stories of Gilgamesh and Enkidu.
1400 B.C.	The Vedic period begins in ancient India.
1000s B.C.	The Phoenicians adopt the North Semitic alphabet.
800s B.C.	The Greeks adopt the Phoenician alphabet.
700s B.C.	The Greek poet Homer writes the *Iliad* and the *Odyssey*.
700s B.C.	Egyptian scribes develop demotic writing.
500s B.C.	The epic period takes place in ancient India.
500s B.C.	The Greeks develop the visual telegraph.
500s B.C.	The Romans adopt an alphabet from the Etruscans and the Greeks.
500 B.C.	The classical period begins in ancient India.
400s B.C.	Drama and playwriting flourish in Greece.
450 B.C.	The art of rhetoric grows in popularity among Greeks.
300s B.C.	Ptolemy Soter begins to build the Library of Alexandria in Egypt.
221 B.C.	Qin Shi Huangdi demands a shared writing system for China.

213 B.C.	Qin Shi Huangdi orders a mass book burning.
190 B.C.	The Greeks develop parchment.
59 B.C.	Roman leader Julius Caesar starts *Acta Diurna* (Daily Events), the world's first daily newspaper.
40 B.C.	Roman historian Gaius Asinius Pollio constructs Rome's first public library.
27 B.C.	Roman emperor Augustus Caesar develops an advanced postal system.
A.D. 105	Ts'ai Lun creates paper from wood pulp.
100s	Chinese clothmakers develop block printing.
100s	The Romans begin to write in cursive.
476	The Roman Empire falls to invaders.
500	Europe enters the Middle Ages.
700s	Chinese papermaking techniques begin to spread across Europe.
1000s	Chinese printers develop movable type.
1300	Europe enters the Renaissance.
1455	Johannes Gutenberg prints his first work with the modern printing press.
1500s	European settlers arrive in the Americas.
1562	Spanish missionaries in Mexico destroy a large collection of Mayan books.
1799	French soldiers discover the Rosetta stone in Egypt.
1800s	Native Americans of the Great Plains refine Plains Sign Language.
1821	Sequoyah completes the Cherokee language syllabary.
1879	The Sanz de Sautuolas discover cave paintings in Altamira, Spain.
1940s	Archaeologists discover Mayan murals at Bonampak in Mexico.
1972	United States scientists launch the *Pioneer 10*.
2006	Archaeologists in San Lorenzo, Mexico, discover the Casajal Block.
2010	Israel announces plans to make the Dead Sea Scrolls available to view online.

GLOSSARY

ABBREVIATION: a shortened form of a written word or phrase

ACRONYM: a word formed from the first letters of words in a compound term

ALPHABET: a set of letters and characters that make up a written language

ARTIFACT: a human-made object, especially one characteristic of a certain group or historical period

CODEX: a book with individual pages

CUNEIFORM: a writing system developed in the ancient Middle East, consisting of wedge-shaped characters

CURSIVE: a style of writing in which letters are connected by flowing lines

DEMOTIC: a simplified form of Egyptian hieroglyphic writing

ENGRAVING: cutting lines or designs into a surface

GRAMMAR: a system of rules about how to use a language

HIERATIC: a simplified form of Egyptian hieroglyphic writing

HIEROGLYPHICS: ancient Egyptian or Mayan picture-writing

IDEOGRAM: a picture or symbol that represents an object or idea

LOGOGRAPHIC: written in symbols that represent words rather than sounds

MANUSCRIPT: a document in which text has been written rather than printed

OSTRACA: a stone used by the ancient Egyptians as a writing surface

PAPYRUS: an Egyptian plant made into paper in ancient times; paper made from the papyrus plant

PARCHMENT: the skin of a sheep or goat made into a writing surface

PHONOGRAM: a symbol used to represent a sound

PICTOGRAM: a picture used to represent an object or idea

PROSE: a style of writing close to ordinary spoken language

SCRIBE: an ancient writer or scholar

SERIFS: short lines on the ends of letters that make reading easier

SYLLABARY: a set of written symbols representing spoken sounds from a language

TELEGRAPH: a system for long-distance communication

VELLUM: the skin of a lamb or calf made into a writing surface

VERSE: a style of writing common to poetry, featuring rhymes and repeated rhythms

SOURCE NOTES

12   Paul G. Bahn, and Jean Vertut, *Journey through the Ice Age* (Berkeley, CA: University of California Press, 1997), 17.

25   Stephen Mitchell, trans., *Gilgamesh: A New English Version* (New York: Free Press, 2004), 71.

28   Richard Parkinson and Stephen Quirke, *Papyrus* (Austin: University of Texas Press, 1995), 11.

29   Leonard H. Lesko, "Hieroglyphics," *World Book Encyclopedia* (Chicago: World Book Inc., 2000).

32   Adolf Erman, *Life in Ancient Egypt*, (New York: Dover Publishing, 1971), 328.

37   Samuel Johnson, *Oriental Religious and Their Relation to Universal Religion* (Boston: James R. Osgood and Company, 1873), 465.

39   Kerry S. Walters and Lisa Portmess, eds., *Religious Vegetarianism* (Albany: State University of New York Press, 2001), 75.

44   Simon Leys, trans., *The Analects of Confucius*, (New York: W.W. Norton and Company, 1997), 29.

44   Ibid.

45   Frances Wood, *China's First Emperor and His Terracotta Warriors* (New York: St. Martin's Press, 2008), 83.

56   Diego de Landa, *Yucatan Before and After the Conquest*, trans. William Gates (New York: Dover Publications, 1978), 170.

56   "Bonampak," *Mayan-Ruins.org*, n.d., http://www.mayan-ruins.org/ bonampak/ (September 21, 2010).

63   Sophocles, *Oedipus the King*, trans. E.D.A. Morshead, (London: Macmillan and Co., 1885), 11.

64   Encyclopedia Britannica Online Reference Center, "History of publishing: vellum and parchment," http://www.library.eb.com.ezproxy.hclib.org/eb/article-28607 (September 22, 2010).

73   Edward Edwards, *Memoirs of Libraries: Including a Handbook of Liberal Economy* (London: Trubner, 1859), 34.

SELECTED BIBLIOGRAPHY

Adkins, Lesley, and Roy A. Adkins. *Handbook to Life in Ancient Rome*. New York: Facts on File, 1994.

Beshore, George. *Science in Ancient China*. New York: Franklin Watts, 1998.

Clark, Ronald W. *Works of Man*. New York: Viking, 1985.

Curtis, Gregory. *The Cave Painters: Probing the Mysteries of the World's First Artists*. New York: Anchor Books, 2007.

Giblin, James Cross. T*he Riddle of the Rosetta Stone: Key to Ancient Egypt*. New York: Harper Collins, 1990.

Haven, Kendall F. *100 Greatest Science Inventions of All Time*. Westport, CT: Libraries Unlimited, 2006.

Hooker, J. T. *Reading the Past: Ancient Writing from Cuneiform to the Alphabet*. Berkeley, CA: University of California Press, 1990.

Ingpen, Robert, and Philip Wilkinson. *Encyclopedia of Ideas That Changed the World: The Greatest Discoveries and Inventions of Human History*. New York: Penguin Books, 1993.

James, Peter, and Nick Thorpe. *Ancient Inventions*. New York: Ballantine Books, 1994.

Joseph, Frank, ed. *Discovering the Mysteries of Ancient America: Lost History and Legends, Unearthed and Explored*. Franklin Lakes, NJ: New Page Books, 2006.

Kirkpatrick, Nadia. *The Maya*. Chicago: Heinemann Library, 2003.

Lauber, Patricia. *Painters of the Caves*. Washington, DC: National Geographic Society, 1998.

Martell, Hazel Mary. *Worlds of the Past: The Ancient Chinese*. New York: New Discovery Books, 1993.

Parkinson, Richard, and Stephen Quirke. *Papyrus*. Austin: University of Texas Press, 1995.

Robinson, Andrew. *The Story of Writing: Alphabets, Hieroglyphs and Pictograms.* New York: Thames and Hudson, 1995.

Saggs, H. W. F. *Civilization Before Greece and Rome.* New Haven, CT: Yale University Press, 1989.

Trumble, Kelly. *The Library of Alexandria.* New York: Clarion Books, 2003.

Walker, C. B. F. *Cuneiform.* Berkeley, CA: University of California Press, 1987.

Woods, Geraldine. *Science in Ancient Egypt.* New York: Franklin Watts, 1998.

FURTHER READING

Childress, Diana. *Johannes Gutenberg and the Printing Press.* Minneapolis: Twenty-First Century Books, 2008.
In this entry in the Pivotal Moments series, readers learn about the history of the Gutenberg's printing press and discover how this invention helped shaped the world.

Dickinson, Rachel. *Tools of the Ancient Romans.* Norwich, VT: Nomad Press, 2006.
Readers can check out this book to discover more technological feats from ancient Rome, learn how the Roman Empire spread across Europe, or try one of many hands-on activities.

Gorrell, Gena K. *Say What? The Weird and Mysterious Journey of the English Language.* Toronto: Tundra Books, 2009.
With help from this book, readers can follow the growth of ancient languages such as Greek and Latin and learn how they influenced to modern-day English.

Jolley, Dan. *Odysseus: Escaping Poseidon's Curse.* Minneapolis: Graphic Universe, 2008.
This graphic novel brings Homer's *Odyssey* to life in an action-packed graphic-novel format.

Opik, E. J. *Ancient China*. New York: DK Children, 2005.
This beautifully illustrated title offers a wealth of information on ancient Chinese technology, art, and culture.

Passport to History series. Minneapolis: Twenty-First Century Books, 2001–2004.
In this series, readers will take trips back in time to ancient China, Egypt, Greece, Rome, and the Mayan civilization. They will learn about people's clothing, transportation, buildings, and other aspects of daily life.

Perl, Lila. *The Ancient Maya*. New York: Franklin Watts, 2005.
This title examines ancient Mayan life and culture.

Schomp, Virginia. *Ancient Mesopotamia: The Sumerians, Babylonians, and Assyrians*. Danbury, CT: Children's Press, 2005. Readers can turn to this book for more information on the different cultures of Mesopotamia and their many technological innovations.

Unearthing Ancient Worlds series. Minneapolis: Twenty-First Century Books, 2008–2009.
This series takes readers on journeys of discovery as archaeologists investigate ruins from the Egyptians, the Inca, the Greeks, and other ancient cultures.

Visual Geography Series. Minneapolis: Twenty-First Century Books, 2003–2011.
Each book in this series examines one country, providing lots of information about its ancient history. The series companion website—vgsbooks.com—offers additional information about each country.

Woods, Michael, and Mary B Woods. Seven Wonders of the Ancient World set. Minneapolis: Twenty-First Century Books, 2009.
This set explores Herodotus's list of the seven ancient wonders as well as magnificent buildings and monuments from ancient Africa, Asia, Central and South America, and North America.

WEBSITES

DISCOVERY CHANNEL: EGYPT
http://www.yourdiscovery.com/egypt/index.shtml
Learn more about reading and writing in ancient Egypt, read up on
Egyptian myths, or play Egypt-themed online games.

HAND PAPERMAKING FOR BEGINNERS
http://newsletter.handpapermaking.org/beginner
If you're interested in making paper by hand, check out this list of
articles about papermaking for curious newcomers.

LIFE: INSIDE LASCAUX
http://www.life.com/image/first/in-gallery/48231/inside-lascaux-rare
-unpublished
Take a virtual tour of magnificent rediscovered cave art from
southwestern France.

ODYSSEY ONLINE: GREECE
http://www.carlos.emory.edu/ODYSSEY/GREECE/home.html
This site from Emory University features more information about
ancient Greek culture, including its legends, its geography, and its
architecture.

UNIVERSITY OF PENNSYLVANIA MUSEUM OF ARCHAEOLOGY AND
ANTHROPOLOGY: WRITE LIKE A BABYLONIAN
http://www.penn.museum/
cgi/cuneiform.cgi
This fun site lets visitors
write their initials in
cuneiform on a virtual clay
tablet.

LERNER SOURCE™

Expand learning beyond the printed
book. Download free, complementary
educational resources for this book
from our website,
www.lernersource.com.

INDEX

Alexandria, Egypt, 63–64
alphabet, 7, 22; Greek, 22, 59–60;
  Latin, 22; North Semitic, 22; origin
  of, 22; Phoenician, 22, 59–60; Proto-
  Canaanite, 22
Altamira caves, 11–12
Americas, 48–57; libraries, 54–55; Maya
  writing systems, 53–55; painted walls
  at Bonampak, 56; quipu, 56–57; sign
  language, 50

Bible, 23, 24, 78
block printing, 46–47
book burning, 45, 55–56
books, 35–37, 41, 47, 54–56, 63–64,
  65–67, 73

cave paintings, 10–15
China, 40–47; block printing, 46–47;
  Confucius, 44; development of ink,
  42; papermaking, 45–46; printing with
  movable type, 47; writing on bark and
  silk, 41
clay tablets, 19–20
codices, 54, 65–67
communication, ancient: in the
  Americas, 48–57; Chinese, 40–47;
  defined, 4–7; Egyptian, 26–33; Greek,
  58–67; Indian, 34–39; Middle Eastern,
  18–25; prehistoric, 8–17; Roman,
  68–75
Confucius, 44
couriers, 75
cuneiform writing, 20–21, 24–25
cursive writing systems, 30, 70

Dark Ages. *See* Middle Ages

Dead Sea Scrolls, 23

Egypt, 26–33; hieroglyphics, 28–29, 33,
  55; papyrus, 26–28, 30, 32; pens, 30;
  scribes, 30, 32–33; writing systems,
  28–30
Epic of Gilgamesh, 24–25

grammar, 38
Greece, 58–67; alphabet, 59–60; codices,
  65–67; development of parchment,
  64–67; library in Alexandria, 63–64;
  oral tradition, 58; runners, 66; scrolls,
  61–62; visual telegraph system, 60
Gutenberg, Johannes, 78

hieroglyphics, 28–29, 33, 53, 55, 78–79
hunter-gatherers, 8–17, 26: cave
  paintings, 10–15; dating cave
  drawings, 13; early spoken
  communication, 9–10; engravings,
  16–17; painting techniques, 14–15

ideograms, 28
India, 34–39; books, 35–37; earliest
  known grammar, 38; road signs,
  38–39; Sanskrit, 35, 36, 38; Vedas,
  35–36
Indus Valley Civilization, 34
ink, 30, 42–43

Latin, 68–70, 77–78
libraries, 54–55, 63–64, 73

marathon, first, 66
Mesopotamia, 18–20, 24–25, 65
Middle Ages, 76–77

Middle East, 18–25; archaeological evidence of writing, 19–20, 22, 23, 25; clay tablets, 19–20; cuneiform, 20–21, 24–25; Dead Sea Scrolls, 23; in pictures, 19, 21; record keeping, 19–20
murals, 57

newspaper, first daily, 74

ostraca, 31

paper, 45–46, 60–61; Chinese papermaking, 45–46, 76–77. *See also* papyrus; parchment
papyrus, 23, 26–28, 30, 32, 46, 60–61, 64, 67
parchment, 46, 64–67
pens, 30, 42, 72
Phoenicians, 7, 22, 59–60
phonograms, 28
pictographs, 19, 21, 40–41, 43, 53, 81–82. *See also* hieroglyphics; totem poles
picture-writing. *See* pictographs
postal system, Roman origins, 7, 75
printing, 46–47, 78

quipu, 56–57
Qui Shi Huangdi, 43, 45

Renaissance, 77–78
rhetoric, 63
road signs, 38–39, 81
Rome, 68–75; copyists, 73–74; couriers and origins of postal system, 75; first daily newspaper, 74; Latin language, 68–70; public libraries, 73; writing, 70–72; writing materials, 72–73
Rosetta stone, 78–79

Sanskrit, 35, 36, 38
scribes, 30, 32–33
scrolls, 51–52. *See also* Dead Sea Scrolls
serifs, 71
sign language, 50
syllabary, Cherokee, 80

technology: ancient roots, 5, 6–7; communication, 6–7; defined, 4–5
telegraph, visual, 60
totem poles, 51
Ts'ai Lun, 45

Vedic age, 35–36

wax tablets, 72–73
writings: Chinese, 40–41, 43; on clay, 19–20; cuneiform, 20–21; demotic, 30, 33, 78; Greek, 59–62, 78–79; hieratic, 30, 33, 78; hieroglyphic, 20–29, 33, 53, 55, 78–79; Mayan, 53–55; pictographs, 19, 21, 40–41, 43, 51, 53, 81–82; Roman, 70–72; on wax tablets, 72–73

ABOUT THE AUTHORS

Michael Woods is a science and medical journalist in Washington, D.C. He has won many national writing awards. Mary B. Woods is a school librarian. Their past books include the fifteen-volume Disasters Up Close series, the seven-volume 7 Wonders of the Ancient World set, and the seven-volume 7 Wonders of the Natural World set. The Woodses have four children. When not writing, reading, or enjoying their grandchildren, the Woodses travel to gather material for future books.

PHOTO ACKNOWLEDGMENTS